Jeannette Gorzala

The Art of Hostile Takeover Defence

IGEL Verlag

Jeannette Gorzala

The Art of Hostile Takeover Defence

1. Auflage 2010 | ISBN: 978-3-86815-285-2

© IGEL Verlag GmbH, 2010. Alle Rechte vorbehalten.

Die Deutsche Nationalbibliothek verzeichnet diesen Titel in der Deutschen Nationalbibliografie. Bibliografische Daten sind unter http://dnb.d-nb.de verfügbar.

IGEL Verlag

Table of contents

1. Abstract

1.1 Purpose and Scope

The market for corporate control had been the playfield of bust-up artists and speculators seeking short-time profits during the 1980s. At that time takeover battles resembled Wild West shootouts, where greenmailers and predators weaponed with Saturday night specials and bear hugs fought against corporate managers and white knights, backed by poison pills and shark repellents. By only taking a short glimpse of the takeover games today you will no longer see legends like Carl C. Icahn or Kirk Kerkorian carve up their junk-bond financed raids for a short lived profit. The landscape of the market for corporate control has changed, as far as now strategy and synergy are the name of the game. Hostile takeovers have become an accepted part of today's M&A activity, however they are still viewed as the most radical and spectacular way to exercise corporate control.

The high level of hostile activity during the 1980s had also encouraged many innovations in the art of hostile takeover defence. Until today anti-takeover defence has reached a very sophisticated level and most companies have erected formidable defences to counter aggressive corporate raiders. A targets anti-takeover arsenal can be segmented into pre-bid and post-bid measures. Prior to the receipt of an unsolicited offer proactive defence strategies can be put in place to decrease the likelihood of a hostile takeover attempt. Once approached by the predator a wide spectrum of post-offer measures can be employed as a direct response to a received hostile takeover bid.

The aim of this thesis is to provide a global perspective on hostile takeover defence during the latest merger wave. The focus lies on firstly determining the most common anti-takeover defence strategies and then in a second step evaluating their effectiveness to ward off corporate raiders. For this purpose the underlying concepts of the formal theory are presented in order to serve as a fundamental basis for an empirical study. In order to underline the theory with empirical evidence a sample of 335 hostile takeover bids launched in the timeframe form January 1, 2003 to December 31, 2008 has been analyzed. The key findings of the study are presented along two vital research questions reflecting the purpose of this thesis.

1.2 Overview and Structure

Apart from the introductory chapter 1, giving a general overview of this thesis' structure and content, this paper consists of four further parts:

- **Chapter 2** provides the vital background information on hostile takeovers that is essential for understanding the involved market mechanisms and the main rationale behind transactions of this kind. In addition a selection of the most common anti-takeover defence strategies is presented, structured in pre-bid and post-bid defence. The aim of this frame of reference is firstly, to introduce the reader to the essential concepts of hostile takeovers and takeover defence mechanisms. Furthermore it shall serve as a basis for the empirical study conducted within the scope of this thesis.

- **Chapter 3** relates to the empirical research performed in order picture the common practice in anti-takeover defence from a global perspective and furthermore determine the success of certain strategies. The chapter outlines the general research approach in section (3.1.) and further contains information on the data sample in (3.2.) and the applied definitions and terminology (3.3.).

- **Chapter 4** is the quintessence of the empirical results. Key insights into the hostile activity during the sixth merger wave between 2003 and 2008 are presented, with a focus on the applied takeover defence and its impact on the transaction success. This aspect is investigated in form of three categories: pre-bid measures, post-bid measures and combined strategy, i.e. e. the company has installed measures to ward off raiders beforehand (pre-bid) and actively reacts against takeover attempts (post-bid). For an in detail view of the topic the analysis comprises information on the geographical and sector distribution as well as transaction volumes.

- **Chapter 5** summarizes the findings based on the empirical research performed. It outlines why and which defence measures had been most frequently applied and further on provides information on their effects on the hostile bid.

The amalgamation of theoretical concepts on the one hand and practical evidence on the other side aims to provide an in-depth view of anti-takeover defence. This study has been conducted on a worldwide basis in order to picture common practice in takeover defence on a global basis.

The illustration below was compiled as guidance to this paper's content and shall provide a consolidated overview of its structure.

Exhibit 1: Overview and structure

Source: Compiled by the author

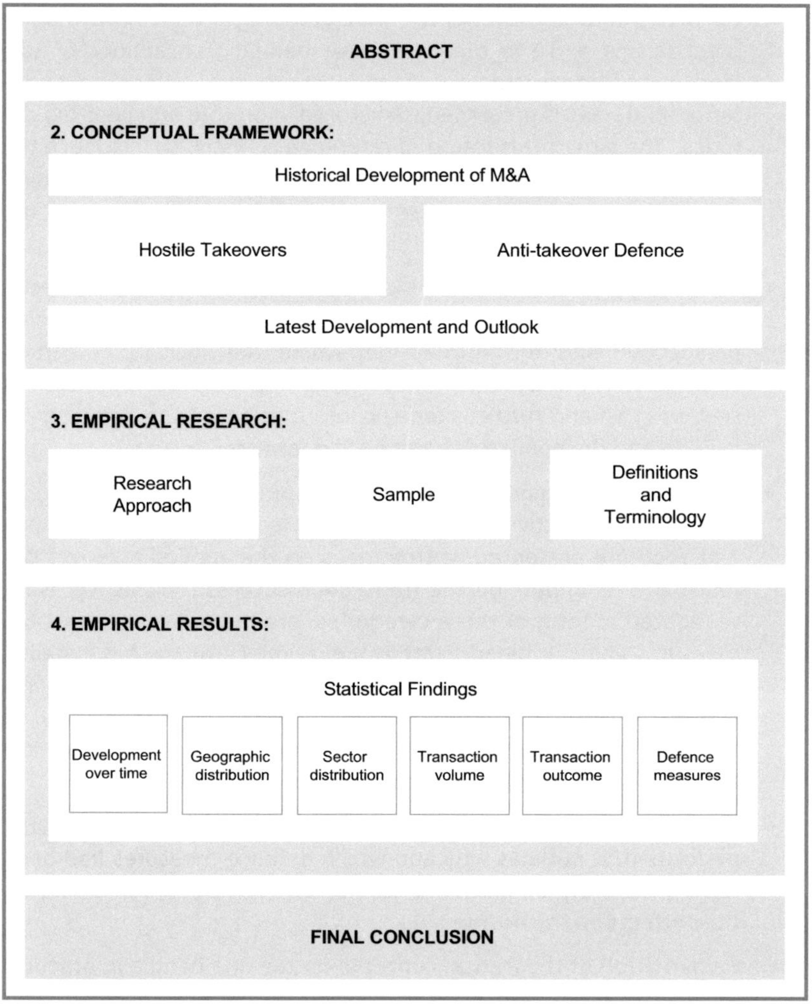

ABSTRACT

2. CONCEPTUAL FRAMEWORK:

Historical Development of M&A

| Hostile Takeovers | Anti-takeover Defence |

Latest Development and Outlook

3. EMPIRICAL RESEARCH:

| Research Approach | Sample | Definitions and Terminology |

4. EMPIRICAL RESULTS:

Statistical Findings

| Development over time | Geographic distribution | Sector distribution | Transaction volume | Transaction outcome | Defence measures |

FINAL CONCLUSION

2 Conceptual Framework

2.1 Historical development of M&A

Waves of mergers and acquisitions have been a feature of corporate history for more than a century. Since the early 1900s six distinct waves of M&A with unique characteristics and outcomes have been observed. This chapter focuses more closely on the later merger periods, as they are more relevant to recent M&A trends. Especially the fourth merger wave during the 1980s, where corporate takeovers reached new levels of hostility, is of great importance within the scope of this thesis as that development was accompanied by many innovations in the area of anti-takeover defence.

The First Wave, 1883 – 1904

The first merger wave occurred after the Depression in 1883, reached its maximum between 1989 and 1902 and came to an end in 1904. A research study conducted by Ralph Nelson (1959) found that primarily eight industries – metals, food products, petroleum products, chemicals, transportation equipment, fabricated metal products, machinery and bituminous coal – accounted for almost two thirds of all mergers during this first wave.[1] This period was predominated by horizontal mergers and industry consolidations, often resulting in an almost monopolistic market structure.

The Second Wave, 1916 – 1929

The second era of M&A had its starting point in 1916 and ended with the stock market crash on October 29, 1929. Towards the end of the first merger period government vigilance had risen and the second wave had to face increased government scrutiny. Anti-trust regulations were put in place as a deterrent to monopolies and the abuse of monopoly power. As a result, large-scale conglomerates and oligopolies were formed during this period. There had been more vertical than horizontal mergers. Many today well-known corporations aroused from the second merger wave, among them General Motors, IBM, John Deere and the Union Carbide Corporation.

The Third Wave, 1965 – 1969

The third merger wave, also known as the conglomerate merger period, featured a historically high level of merger activity brought about by a booming economy. According to the Federal Trade Commission (FTC), 80 percent of all mergers between 1965 and 1975 were conglomerate merg-

---

[1] See Nelson, R. (1959)

ers. For instance, in the 1960s ITT acquired Avis Rent a Car, Sheraton Hotels, Continental Banking and other diverse enterprises such as restaurant chains, consumer credit agencies, home building companies and airport parking firms. Apart from prestigious conglomerate firms like ITT, Ling-Temco-Vought and Litton Industries corporations of varying sizes engaged in a diversification strategy.

The Fourth Wave, 1984 – 1989

Although corporate raiders existed before the 1980s, the fourth merger wave between 1984 and 1989 was unique in that it featured predators, armed with a large arsenal of junk bond financing to attack some of the largest corporations. By 1908 hostile takeovers had become an acceptable path of corporate expansion and gained status as highly profitable speculative activity. Corporations as well as speculative partnerships engaged in takeover games with the aim of achieving extremely high returns within a short period of time. Although the number of hostile transactions with respect to the total number of takeovers was not high, the relative percentage of hostile takeovers in the total transaction value was substantial. The total consideration paid in acquisitions rose sharply during the fourth M&A era. From 1974 to 1986 the number of USD 100 million transactions increased more than 23 times. This was the period during which corporate raiders like Boone Pickens, Carl Icahn and Kirk Kerkorian, to name only a few of them, challenged their selected targets with two-tier, boot-strap, bust-up, junk-bond hostile tender offers until the poison pill levelled the playfield in the mid-1980s.

This long period of economic expansion came to an end in 1989 and was followed by a brief recession in 1990. As a consequence of the economic slowdown, some of the high-profile leveraged deals had been unravelled. The USD 25 billion RJR Nabisco Leveraged Buy Out (LBO) and the collapse of the junk bond market marked the end of the fourth merger wave.

The Fifth Wave, 1993 – 2000

After the collapse of the junk bond market the number of mergers and acquisitions began to increase again in 1992. During the fifth merger wave from 1993 to 2000 strategically driven transactions that were financed rather by an increased use of equity prevailed. [2] In the time period between 1991 and 2006 there had been more transactions annually than in any other period over the past century, averaging almost 21,000 transactions per year.

---

[2]   See Gaughan, P. A. (2002), pp. 23-54

Six of the ten largest mergers in history occurred during this merger wave in the two-year period between 1998 and 2000 (see table 1). The global perspective on competition in combination with a relatively restrained antitrust environment led to combinations, such as the mergers of Vodafone and Mannesmann, AOL and Time Warner, Exxon and Mobile, Citibank and Travelers, Chrysler and Daimler Benz, and Boeing and McDonnell Douglas. The worldwide volume of mergers steadily increased up to an amount of USD 3.3 trillion, compared with a rather modest sum of USD 342 billion in 1992.

After the burst of the Dot-com Bubble volumes and values of transactions dipped for three years after the end of the fifth M&A wave in 2000, when the number of transactions had reached a record high of approximately 29,500 deals. There was a dramatic slowdown in the overall M&A sector, especially in the telecommunications, media and technology (TMT) industry. The NASDAQ had fallen more than 50 percent from its high and many TMT stocks even experienced a plunge of almost 98 percent.[3]

Rank	Transaction Value (in USDbn)	Year	Bidder	Target
1	183.00	1999	Vodafone Airtouch	Mannesmann
2	164.75	2000	America Online	Time Warner
3	90.84	2007	Royal Bank of Scotland, Banco Santander, Fortis	ABN Amro
4	90.00	1999	Pfitzer	Warner-Lambert
5	77.20	1998	Exxon	Mobil
6	75.96	2000	Glaxo Wellcome	SmithKline Beecham
7	74.56	2004	Royal Dutch Petroleum	Shell Transport & Trading
8	73.00	1999	Citicorp	Travelers Group
9	72.04	2001	Comcast	AT&T Broadband & Internet Services
10	72.67	2006	AT&T	BellSouth Corporation

Table 1: Largest M&A Deals, 1999-2007
Source: Institute of Mergers, Acquisitions and Alliances (retrieved on 17.06.2007),
CNN Money, company information

The Sixth Wave, 2004

The sixth M&A wave, which started in 2003 after the Internet Bubble at the turn of the century and the subsequent economic downturn, is mainly about consolidation. Consolidation deals as a percentage of the total value of transactions surged from 48.7 percent in the period between

---

3   See Lipton, M. (2006), p. 6

1999 and 2000 to 71.4 percent in 2006. That trend had been facilitated by globalization, a more liberal regulatory environment in certain sectors and bulging M&A war chests. The number of mega deals over USD 1 billion added up to 460 transactions in 2006, just slightly below the record high of 470 deals in 2000.

Moreover, private equity firms started to play an increasingly important role. During the time period from 1996 to 2006 their share of the total deal volume increased from 6 to 14 percent. The portion of PE-transactions as a percentage of the total transaction value increased even more dramatically from 8 to 24 percent in the same time frame. In fact, the involvement of private equity firms measured in absolute terms is striking. The total value of PE-deals had soared from USD 160 billion in 2000 to USD 650 billion in 2006. Although private equity houses had fuelled the sixth merger wave, accounting for approximately one quarter of all deals, mainly strategic buyers had driven it.[4]

2.2 Hostile Takeovers

2.2.1 Definition

Hostile takeovers are also referred to as *unfriendly* takeovers, *defended* takeovers or *contested* takeovers.[5] In those takeover situations the target company receives an unsolicited unfriendly offer for all or a fraction of the outstanding shares at a stated tender price from a corporate raider, who aspires to acquire at least a 50 percent holding in the target company in order to achieve a majority representation on the board. Unwelcome bids are often perceived to at least threaten a few of the target's stakeholders and therefore induce extensive defensive reactions by the management of the target corporation. In contrast friendly takeovers are mostly considered as win-win situations for both the bidder and the target by creating synergies.

It has been criticized that all expressions for unsolicited takeover offers have a negative judgemental denotation. This is probably because of the circumstance that some stakeholders are likely to be disadvantaged by the transaction, whereas friendly takeovers are believed to increase the target's as well as the bidder's wealth. However, in light of the rationale of the market of corporate control the general negative associations with

---

[4] See Cools, K., Gell, J., Kengelbach, J., Roos, A. (2007), p. 9
[5] See Strazzer, R. (1993), p. 19

hostile takeovers seem incorrect, as the removal of an inefficient target management team creates gains from hostile takeovers.

According to Schwert (2000), the term "hostility" can be defined in different ways. Generally hostility is perceived when the approached target corporation aggressively rejects the public offer received. Moreover it can be noted that hostility is closely interlinked with takeover negotiations that are still far from completion. Often companies are already in the process of confidential negotiations before the public is informed about the potential transaction. In many cases the first public announcement is of a successful completed negotiation. Given this information the deal would be perceived as friendly, even if the privately held negotiations in their early stage had seemed hostile to the public. Though, private negotiations may also break down as one of the involved parties decides that public information about the planned takeover offer would enhance its bargaining position. On the one hand bidders might reveal their intentions in order to put the target's management board under shareholder pressure, but also targets might reveal a takeover attempt to attract alternative offers and encourage a bidding war.

Therefore clearly distinguishing between friendly and hostile transactions is rather complex, as public announcements of takeover attempts are an integrated part of negotiating strategies. Furthermore, as with any negotiation, circumstances change over time and with them also the attitudes and expectations of the parties involved. Therefore many transactions that initially might have seemed hostile resulted in friendly negotiated settlements. [6]

2.2.2 Economic rationale

From the viewpoint of the market for corporate control hostile takeovers are seen as an instrument to exercise management control, which is to bring about disciplinary effects on management. On the other side they can also be viewed as a tool to accelerate market and industry consolidation. From a corporation point of view, however, the economic rationale for a hostile takeover should be equal to the motives for friendly takeovers, meaning that the transaction must produce economic gains and increase shareholder wealth. Therefore M&A activity has many drivers, of which the most important ones are illustrated in exhibit 2. They can generally be segmented in strategic motives, operational motives and management control.

---

[6]   See Schwert (2000), pp. 2599, 2600

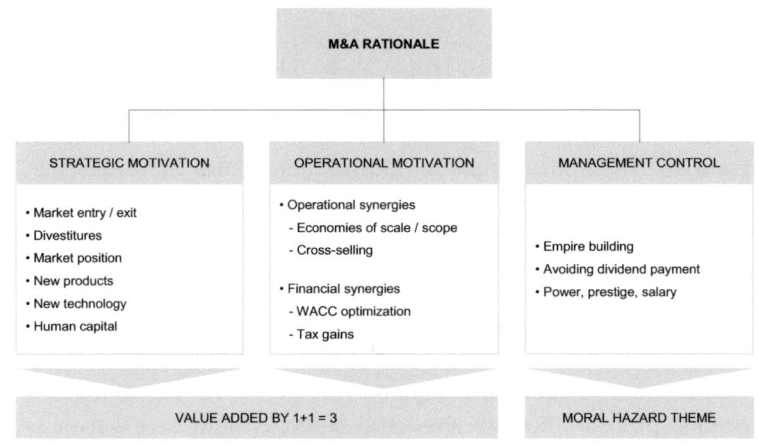

Source: Compiled by the author

2.2.3.1 Strategic and Operational Motivations

While the creation of synergies is one of the primary motives of mergers and acquisitions, they can be based upon a strategic and an operational level. A popular definition of synergy is "one plus one equals three", or expressed more technically, the synergy value is the amount by which the value of the combined entities exceeds the sum value of the two stand-alone enterprises. Generally synergies can be segmented in operating and financial synergies.

In respect to strategic motivations it has to be noted that M&A generally plays and important role in corporate strategy. Corner stones in a broad spectrum of possible strategic goals a company may want to achieve through a merger or acquisition are market entry or exit, divestitures of businesses, improvement of market position, development of new products, and access to new technology or human capital. All these actions should contribute to a company's long-term success by creating a more competitive company in the marketplace through an optimal allocation of resources, including the realization of synergies on a strategic level.

In respect to operational synergies, they can be further segmented into operating and financial synergies. Operating synergies comprise cost reduction, by eliminating redundancies in administration, production and logistics as well as revenue enhancement, achieved through cross-selling and complementary matching of strengths and weaknesses. Financial synergy refers to the possibility of optimizing the cost of capital by combining one or more entities and potential tax gains.

2.2.3.2 Management Control

According to Schwert (2000) the particular intention to establish a more efficient management in poorly run companies is probably the main factor that differentiates a hostile from a friendly takeover.[7] Apart from this differentiation between hostile and friendly takeovers, the change of management is often necessary as managers are the shareholder's agents, but both parties have their own interests, leading to serious conflicts between them in terms of the right choice of the best corporate strategy. For example, a great number of top-level executives strive at constantly enlarging the business. One reason for this development is the association of power and prestige with the size of the firm. In addition many compensation schemes budget huge financial awards for managers that enlarge their enterprises (e.g. compensation tied to assets under administration). Empire building, however, is seen as unhealthy for a corporation, as managers are more concerned with expanding business units, their staffing levels and the value of assets under control than with optimally allocating resources and implementing strategies to benefit shareholders. As a consequence executives may not necessarily select the corporate actions required to provide the best growth opportunity for the corporation and its shareholders. When agency costs, i.e. costs of monitoring management and efficiency losses because of conflicts of interests, are large, the threat of takeovers can reduce them. Empirical research by Martin and McConnell (1991) validates the argument, that takeovers play an important role in controlling corporate managers and aligning their incentives with shareholder's interests.

2.2.3 Takeover Process

A hostile takeover, as every takeover, can be modelled as a series of operations, performed sequentially in order to bring about a specified result, in this case the acquisition of a company (see exhibit 3). Here the peculiarities of a hostile takeover situation are pointed out based on the general acquisition process from the bidder's point of view.

Upon a detailed analysis of the bidder's strengths, weaknesses, financial performance and competitive situation target requirements, for instance

---

[7]   See Schwert (2000), p. 2599

revenue, size, region, industry, etc. are defined. By defining the acquisition criteria and goals this first step is an important module of the acquisition process as a whole as the course for a successful takeover is set. Within the second step a target company is identified and a long-list of potential acquisition objects is compiled. Mostly, professional M&A advisors are involved, which develop a short-list of targets in coordination with the bidder. The advisor then approaches the targeted companies in order to sound out the situation and possible sale or cooperation intentions and therefore allows the bidder to remain nameless, in case the potential target should not be interested. If the advisor attracts the targeted company's interest, further proceedings are defined and the first contact between target and bidder is established. One of the most important steps in a takeover process is the due diligence, where the bidder extensively analyzes the target company. In the data room the potential acquirer has access to highly sensitive and most relevant information. After a detailed analysis of the company as well as the risk of an acquisition the company valuation is performed, serving as a basis for the bidder's purchase offer. After the offer is presented, negotiations follow. A successful takeover process is complete after the purchase agreement has been signed and the deal is closed.[8]

Exhibit 3: Process overview (bidder's perspective)

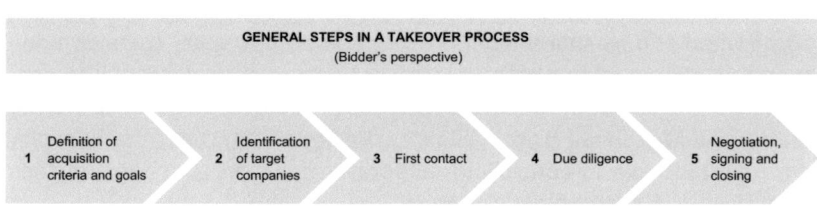

Source: Adapted from Raupach, G. (2007), p. 209

The first two steps, i.e. the definition of acquisition goals and the identification of a target are identical with the general proceedings in regular takeover situations. Stage three, the first contact, is widely different, as the hostile bidder seeks to consummate the acquisition within the shortest possible time period, as other bidders may enter the playing field or the target company can mount stronger defences. Typical approaches of a potential acquirer could be firstly, the purchase of shares directly in the

---

[8] See Raupach, G. (2007), pp. 209-211

market, secondly, an offer directly to the target's board of directors and in the third place a tender offer directly to target shareholders. The direct purchase of shares in the market is rarely used, as under most takeover regulations the bidder must notify the national financial market authority upon surpassing a defined percent stake in the target. These regulations were put in place to limit the element of surprise. With an offer directly to the target's board of directors bidders seek to gain its support in order to persuade the target to drop its defences. The most common forms are the Saturday night special, the bear hug and tender offers, whereby each varies in price, publicity and validity period. The Saturday night special defined as a surprising offer to the target board, left open only for a brief period of time. A bear hug in contrast is an offer made to the board without a concurrent public announcement. Tender offers are an invitation to target shareholders to tender or submit their shares for sale to the buyer. Typically such offers state a price, form of payment and length of time that the offer will be valid.

Another feature of a hostile takeover process in contrast to friendly acquisitions is that there is no due diligence prior to the acquisition. Therefore the potential acquirer has to endure a severe lack of highly important information together with a higher acquisition risk. Regarding negotiations, two scenarios are possible. Some hostile takeovers might be settled friendly and be recommended by the target's board after all, for instance because of an increased offer price. The other case is that the target company disapproves the acquisition to the end. In step five, the deal completion, there is again no difference between a hostile takeover and a friendly situation.

2.3   Anti-Takeover Defence

The high level of hostile activity during the 1980s encouraged many innovations in the art of hostile takeover defence. Because of the increased application of financial resources by threatened corporations, defence strategies became quite elaborate and more difficult to penetrate. At the end of the fourth M&A era, anti-takeover defence had reached a very sophisticated level. Top-tier investment banks provided teams of specialists, who together with the company's management erected formidable defences to counter the aggressive corporate raiders of the fourth merger wave. After installing a broad spectrum of defence tools, teams of investment bankers and legal advisors were ready on demand to advise the target's management on the proper actions to take to fend off the potential acquirer. By the 1990s most of the large corporations had some form of anti-takeover defence in place.

The vast number of defence measures can be structured along many dimensions. Within the frame of this paper the array of anti-takeover defence is divided into two categories: pre-bid and post-bid measures. Pre-bid defence strategies are put in place to discourage potential bidders from making an attempt and are designed to reduce the likelihood of a successful hostile takeover. Reactive post-bid measures are employed as a direct response to a received hostile takeover bid.

Exhibit 4: Characteristics of pre-/post-bid defence

PROACTIVE VS. REACTIVE TAKEOVER DEFENCE

PRE ——————→ TAKEOVER BID ——————→ POST

PRE-BID Defence	POST-BID Defence
• Increase the company's market value • Therefore reduction of the potential (unfriendly) bidder's value gain • Increase the unfriendly bidder's risk • Prearrangement of an emergency defence strategy	• Increase of bid premium / improvement of takeover conditions (e.g. employment guaranty, etc.) • More difficult takeover process • Increase of acquisition costs and risks • Delay transaction closure
Proactive prevention of takeover attempts	Defensive response to a received takeover offer

Source: Compiled by the author

Further on pre-bid defence can be segmented in two sub-categories: corporate charter amendments and other shark repellents. Anti-takeover charter amendments become effective only if a takeover attempt is presented, their instalment however has taken place prior to the receipt of the hostile offer. The term "shark repellent" refers to any measures taken by the target in order to fend off an unwanted or hostile takeover. Exhibit 6 provides an overview of the classification of hostile takeover defence applied within the frame of this thesis.

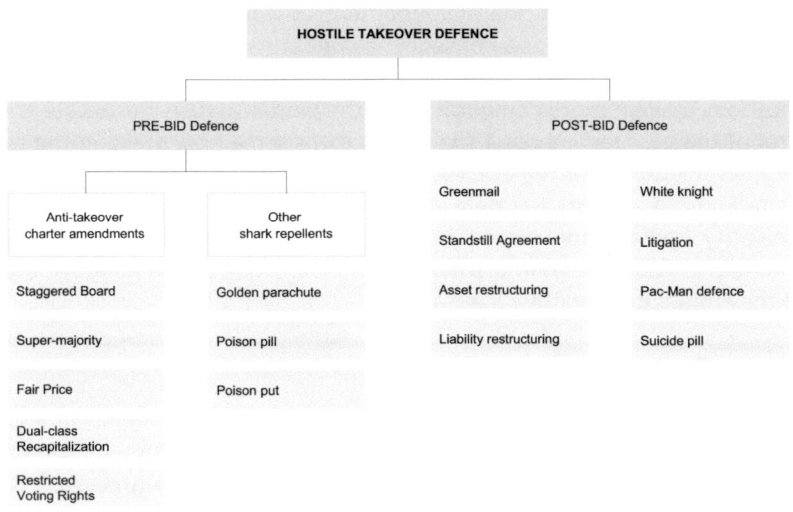

This chapter shall serve as a tactical perspective on hostile takeover defence and introduce a selection of the most common anti-takeover tools in a target's arsenal. Anticipating the impact of such techniques is of significant importance, as they have a great impact on the speed of closure, likelihood of the transactions' success and cost or profit to the bidder. Unfriendly takeovers may only represent a small percentage of the total M&A activity, but nevertheless most large firms have installed some form of defence system. Takeover barriers are rather the rule than the exception and therefore a fundamental knowledge of the most frequently applied measures is vital.

2.3.1 Pre-Bid Defence

This section illustrates proactive defence strategies that are typically installed prior to a takeover offer with the aim of discouraging potential bidders from attacking. They are summarized in table 2 that firstly contains a short description of the type of defence and in addition briefly outlines the impact of the particular measure.

2.3.1.1 Staggered Board

Staggered or classified board amendments divide the board into groups (usually three) so that as a consequence directors are elected fractionally each year (e.g. each year only one third of the directors is elected). Classifications make it more complicated for the bidder to gain immediate control of the company, even if the bidder owns a majority stake in the target, as it's ability to replace the entire board at once is delayed. Staggered boards are a moderately effective pre-bid defence measure. As the majority holder is prevented from obtaining control of the board and therefore is not able to implement significant changes immediately, even if they might be urgently necessary.[9]

2.3.1.2 Super-Majority Provisions

After comparing state corporation laws of a wide range of countries it can be noted that most laws require a minimum approval of either 51% or two thirds of the voting shares for mergers. Super-majority provisions are corporate charter provisions that require approval by an extra-large majority of votes, regularly more than 80% of the outstanding share's voting power. This charter amendment intends to empower a minority of shareholders so they can protect their interests in case of a strong attack. Furthermore the bidder is delayed in accomplishing the deal as it takes more time to amass a super-majority. Typically these amendments are accompanied by lock-in provisions that require the same super-majority to change the amendment and related anti-takeover provisions. Generally M&A advisors recommend a modification of pure super-majority amendments because of their negative effect on the board's flexibility in any takeover negotiations. Therefore such provisions nowadays are relatively rare. Pure super-majority amendments have been either replaced by similar provisions (e.g. triggered by board action or type of takeover offer) or include board-out clauses that give the management board discretion to abolish the super-majority requirement.[10]

According to Linn and McConnell (1983), the announcement results in a five percent reduction of shareholder's wealth.[11] However, Johnson and Rao found that in a long-term perspective super-majority decisions as well as other anti-takeover charter amendments have no negative impact on the target company itself or the stockholders.

---

9   See Ruback, R. S. (1988), p. 56 – 57
10 See Jarrell, G. A., Poulsen, A. B. (1987), p. 131
11 See Linn, S. C., McConnell, J. J. (1983)

2.3.1.3 Fair Price Amendment

Fair price amendments were designed as a measure to prevent two-tier takeover attempts, as they require the bidder to pay a so-called fair price for all purchased shares. The fair price can be determined in several ways (e.g. by formula). Most commonly the fair price equals the highest price paid by the bidder for any shares purchased in the target firm during a specified period. Nevertheless the bid may need to meet additional requirements (e.g. a premium over the current market price). Generally two-tier takeover offers are structured to purchase a controlling stake in the company at a premium, whereas the remaining minority is bought at a discount, with the aim of stampeding current stockholders into selling.[12]

2.3.1.4 Dual-Class Recapitalization

Dual-class recapitalization plans create two classes of a company's equity with different voting rights and therefore represent a derivation from the normal one share/one vote rule. Ownership of equity is separated from the ownership of voting rights. Superior voting stock is typically extended to management and company founders and characterized by superior voting privilege and lower dividends. As a result management enjoys increased control over corporate affairs and has the ability to block hostile propositions. The inferior common stock by contrast has limited voting rights but therefore a preferential claim to dividend payment.[13]

2.3.1.5 Restricted Voting Rights

Several companies amend their charters to include restricted voting rights provisions, separating significant shareholders from their voting rights. Usually stockholders with a stake in the target company exceeding 15 percent or 20 percent lose their voting right when it comes to making decisions about accepting or rejecting takeover offers.[14]

2.3.1.6 Golden Parachute

Golden parachutes are additions to existing executive employment contracts that represent separation provisions to managers under a change-of-control clause. The employees are granted certain benefits, commonly involving severance pay, bonuses in cash or stock options, pension, lump

---

[12]   See Bruner, R. F. (2004), p. 835
[13]   See Loh, C., Rathinasamy, R. S. (1995)
[14]   See Ivkovic, I. (2008a)

sum payments or other executive benefits. In order to obtain remuneration from the golden parachute the corporation must have undergone some type of "change in control" (e.g. purchase of a substantial block of outstanding stock, a change in the majority of the Board of Directors or acquisition of the company) and furthermore termination of the executive's employment must have taken place.

According to Lambert and Larcker (1985) only a small percentage of senior-level executives, relative to the number of managerial employees usually participate in the contract. The average of executives covered by golden parachutes accounts for 9.7 percent. However, the number of participating executives as a percentage of all directors and officers almost accounts for one third, representing a quite large number of senior-level managers deciding on the company's response to a takeover offer.[15]

Jensen and Ruback (1983) provide considerable evidence for the hypothesis that the target company's shareholders gain profit when their firm is acquired. Due to their analysis target shareholders on average earn abnormal returns of 20 percent for a successful mergers and 30 percent for successful tender offers.[16] For the target firm's management in contrast an unfriendly takeover involves two major downside risks. Firstly, in case of termination of employment, the manager does not receive wages until he finds a new employment and secondly, he as well loses non-pecuniary benefits of his position, most notably power and prestige. In order to help reduce the conflict of interest between shareholders and managers in change-of-control situations, golden parachutes are provided to executives. In most cases executives receive large dollar amounts, however the cost usually accounts for less than 1% of the total takeover value.

The rationale is to reduce the manager's potential loss in case of a takeover and therefore reduce resistance from approving an acquisition. Apart from interest alignment another argument in favour of golden parachutes is the encouragement to firm-specific investments in the shareholders' best interests. However, Jensen (1988) found that contracts that award inappropriately high payments to a large group of executives will reduce efficiency and harm shareholders by transferring wealth to managers and boosting acquisition costs.[17]

---

[15] See Lambert, R. A., Larcker, D. F. (1985), pp. 180, 181
[16] See Jensen, M., Ruback, R. S. (1983)
[17] See Jensen (1988), p. 31

2.3.1.7 Poison Pill

In 1982 the poison pill was created by the M&A lawyer Martin Lipton as a response to tender-based hostile takeover offers. As a result of the increasing trend in corporate raids in the 1980s this anti-takeover measure became very popular. Nevertheless many jurisdictions other than the U.S. consider this strategy as illegal or at least pace restraints on its use (e.g. Great Britain, Germany, etc.).

Poison pills are preferred stock rights plans usually using securities authorized by stockholders with conditions determined by the board prior to issuance. They provide stockholders with an inactive right to obtain preferred stock, which is triggered in the event of a tender offer for a large fraction of the firm, usually 30 percent, or after the ownership of one single stockholder exceeds 20 percent of the company. If the board of directors does not redeem the rights within a short time window after the triggering event, they can be exercised.

In general two different plans for using exercised rights can be distinguished. Firstly, flip-in plans, where the issuing firm repurchases the rights from its shareholders by a substantial premium, whereas the bidding firm or the triggering shareholder is excluded from the buyback. As a result the bidders equity position in the target company will be diluted. Secondly, flip-over plans, when the target company issues rights as a pro rata dividend on the common stock to its shareholders. The rights become exercisable and separate from the common stock upon a specific defined event, which is typically the announcement of an intent to acquire a specified percentage of the issuer's stock by a prospective acquirer. Although the rights are then exercisable, and remain so for the duration of their specified life (typically ten years), they remain out of the money. Because they are traded separately from the issuer's common stock, however, an acquirer remains subject to the pill's poisonous effects even if a majority of the target's shareholders accept the bidder's offer. The pill's flip-over feature typically is triggered if, following the acquisition of a specified percentage of the target's common stock, the target is subsequently merged into the acquirer or one of its affiliates. In this case the holder the right becomes entitled to purchase common stock of the acquiring company at a steep discount to market, thereby impairing the acquirer's capital structure and drastically diluting the interest of the acquirer's other stockholders.[18]

---

[18] See Bainbridge, S. M. (2002), pp. 11-13

Both forms of poison pills are among the most effective anti-takeover defences in the target's arsenal.[19] As a matter of fact, most poison pills are designed in the belief that they will never be triggered. In 2001 CFO Magazine reported that since 1997, for every company with an installed poison pill that successfully resisted a corporate raid, there had been 20 companies protected by poison pills that had accepted a takeover offer.[20]

2.3.1.8 Poison Put

As a consequence of the RJR-Nabisco leveraged buyout in December 1988 bond values declined. This development stimulated the development of a at that time new merger defence – poison puts.[21] When change of control occurs poison puts trigger debt repayments at or above par value. As a consequence, takeover attempts are discouraged by forcing the bidder to provide more financing and an eventual premium for the target company's debt.[22]

Summary overview of common pre-bid defence strategies

Defence Strategy	Description	Impact
Anti-takeover charter amendments:		
Staggered board	The board is classified into three equal groups, whereby only one group is elected each year.	Even after obtaining a majority of shares the bidder cannot immediately obtain control of the target company.
Super-majority provision	For reaching an approval of a merger a high percentage of shares is required, typically 80%.	An increase the number of shares is needed to obtain control of the target in hostile takeover situations.
Fair price amendment	All shareholders must receive a uniform, fair price	Prevents two-tier takeover offers.
Dual-class recapitalization	Higher-class equity with superior voting privilege and lower dividends as well as common equity with preferential claim on dividends is extended	Management holding superior equity is able to block hostile propositions.
Restricted voting rights	Shareholders who own more than a specified stake in the target company have no voting rights, unless approved by the targets board.	It is more difficult to obtain a large stake in the target within a relative short period of time.

---

[19] See Ruback, R. S. (1988), pp. 58 – 60
[20] See Frieswick, K. (2001)
[21] See Copeland, T. E., Weston, J. F., Shastri, K. (2005), p. 795
[22] See Bruner, R. F. (2004), p. 842

Other shark repellents:

Golden parachute	An agreement to the effect that the target's management in case of job loss resulting from a takeover will receive significant provisions.	Increase in acquisition costs.
Poison pill	Two common types: a) *Flip-In Pill:* allows shareholders of the target company to purchase more shares at a discount price b) *Flip-Over Pill:* allows shareholders of the target company to buy shares in the acquirer significantly below their market price after the takeover	Aims at prohibitively making hostile tender offers expensive
Poison put	The target's bondholders have the right to sell back their bonds at a pre-determined price (put price usually set above par) if a hostile takeover triggers a change of control.	Increase in acquisition costs.

Table 2: Summary of pre-bid defence strategies
Source: Adapted from Ruback, R. S. (1988), pp. 54, 55

2.3.2 Post-Bid Defence

Should pre-takeover defence fail, companies can further on respond with several post-bid anti-takeover actions that can be directly aimed at a specific bidder. Table 3 summarizes these post-offer defensive responses.

2.3.2.1 Greenmail

As the name greenmail implies, this defence measure, like blackmail, pays the intruder to leave. In a situation in which a corporate raider owns a large block of stock in the target company, the target is forced to repurchase its own shares from the acquirer at a substantial premium in order to prevent a hostile takeover. However, the repurchase offer is not extended to other shareholders. Due to that fact greenmail prompted sharp criticism and legal disputes aroused with shareholders who did not obtain the large premium for their shares. As a result some companies prohibited greenmail payments by charter amendments and a 50 percent tax on greenmail profits was introduced by an amendment to the U.S. Internal Revenue Code.[23] This anti-takeover measure, also known as "Bon Voyage Bonus" or "Goodbye Kiss" was a very popular measure during the fourth M&A-wave during the 1980s.

---

[23]   See Ivkovic, I. (2008b)

2.3.2.2 Standstill Agreement

In takeover situations a standstill agreement restricts the raider's ability to acquire further shares in the target firm. The purpose of the agreement is to limit the potential raider's ownership for a specified period of time and thereby provide the target with an extended time frame to build up other takeover defence measures. These agreements, at least temporarily, eliminate a potential bidder.

Dann and DeAngelo (1983) show that standstill agreements are associated with a statistically significant decline in stock prices of about four percent.[24] Furthermore empirical results by Mikkelson and Ruback (1986) find that negative returns in response to targeted repurchases are much greater when accompanied by standstill agreements. However, the stock price decline could also simply be the market's expression of disappointment, as the expected takeover did not take place.[25]

2.3.2.3 Asset Restructuring

Asset restructuring as an anti-takeover defence summarizes all acquisitions and divestitures used, in order to change the target company's asset structure as a strategy to ward off hostile bids. Such tactics include the divestiture of an asset that the bidder absolutely wants, purchasing assets the acquirer does not want or buying assets that are likely to trigger regulatory problems (e. g. anti-trust, etc.).

Divestitures of resources the bidder had hoped to take advantage of (e.g. patents, licenses, land, etc.) make the company less attractive to the corporate raider and reduce the price the bidder is willing to pay. As an ultima ratio measure the defending target might implement the crown jewel defence and sell off its most valuable key assets. In addition any asset sale can serve as funding for extraordinary dividends, greenmail payment or other defence tactics.

The acquisition of assets, making the company a less desirable target, is another form of defensive anti-takeover restructuring. Especially in regulated industries (e.g. banking, broadcasting, transportation, etc.) asset purchases can have significant impact on the success of a transaction as horizontal acquisitions are limited by regulations. [26]

---

[24] See Dann, L. Y., DeAngelo, H. (1983)
[25] See Mikkelson, W., Ruback, R. S. (1986)
[26] See Bruner, R. F. (2004), pp. 847-848

Research conducted by Dann and DeAngelo (1986) provides statistical significant evidence that the announcement of asset restructuring results in the decline of shareholder wealth and a reduction in stock prices of two percent.[27]

2.3.2.4 Liability Restructuring

On the one hand the target company can issue voting securities and thereby increase the number of shares required by the bidder for obtaining control of the target company. Generally these new securities are placed in friendly hands supporting the target's current management board. Alternatively the number of publicly traded shares can be reduced by repurchase. This approach makes it more difficult for the potential acquirer to buy the amount of shares needed to obtain control of the target. Often such buybacks are financed by debt issues in order to make the company even less attractive for the predator.

Further on a leveraged recapitalization can be an attractive defence tool, as it involves taking on huge debts and paying target shareholders a large one-time dividend. After the cash is paid out to the stockholders a weak and highly leveraged target is left behind. In the event of an acquisition the bidder would assume a large debt burden from the target. Additionally in highly leveraged recapitalizations a couple of debt provisions include poison puts, triggered upon a change of control. As a consequence the bidding company must be prepared to repay the target's debt immediately upon acquisition.[28]

2.3.2.5 White Knight

A white knight is a friendly potential acquirer sought out by the target company that is threatened by a corporate raider. Generally horizontal or vertical peers of the target firm, motivated by prospective synergies or aiming at the stabilization of strategic relationships are considered as white knights because of the good strategic fit. However, a white knight can also act on behalf of a purely financial rational.

In contrast to a white knight as a friendly acquirer, the white squire merely purchases a large stake in the target, but without taking control of the company. Thereby the company can block a hostile takeover. Usually the white squire agrees to vote in alignment with the target's manage-

---

[27]   See Dann, L. Y., DeAngelo, H. (1986)
[28]   See Bruner, R. F. (2004), p. 847

ment and accepts a temporary limitation of its stake held in the target for a certain period of time.

The white knight/squire defence aims at pre-empting a hostile bidder of control and by partnering with a friendly third party.[29] The table below shortly outlines examples for transactions involving white knights that attracted public attention in recent years.

Year	Target	Bidder	White Knight	Deal Description
2008	ImClone Systems	Bristol-Meyers Squibb	Eli Lilly	In order to ward of the unsolicited proposal of Bristol-Meyers Squibb, the EUR 70 per share offer of Eli Lilly had been approved.
2006	Germanischer Lloyd (GL)	Bureau Veritas	Guenter Herz	To avoid the hostile takeover by Bureau Veritas the private investor G. Herz acquired 100% of GL's share capital for a total consideration of EUR 550m.
2006	Schering	Merck	Bayer	Bayer acted as a white knight to Schering; Merck's EUR 77 per share hostile takeover offer was contested by Bayer's EUR 86 white knight bid.
2006	Myojo Foods	Steel Partners	Nissin Foods	Nissin launched a friendly USD 314m bid to prevent Myojo from an acquisition by the U.S. hedge fund Steel Partners
2003	The Canada Life Assurance Company	Manulife	Great-West Lifeco	The "white knight" competing offer of Great-West Lifeco, valuing the target EUR 4,458m had been accepted.

Table 3: Examples of white knights
Source: Mergermarket, company information

2.3.2.6 Litigation

According to Jarrell (1985) in approximately one third of all tender offers extended in the time period from 1962 to 1980, target companies filed some sort of lawsuit (e. g. fraud, violation of antitrust or securities regulations, etc.) against the potential acquirer. On the basis of Jarrell's research two main purposes of litigations as a takeover defence can be identified. Firstly, through the delay of the bidder, competing bidders are encouraged to launch an offer. Jarrell found that competing bids occurred in 62 percent of all tender offers including litigation, whereas in the case of tender offers without litigation only 11 percent received competing bids. Secondly, litigation is said to prompt tenderers to raise their bid to induce the target to drop the suit and to avoid legal expenses. However, this hypothesis is not validated through Jarrell's study, reporting that the stock

---

[29] See Bruner, R. F. (2004), p. 848

price effect associated with filing a lawsuit is about zero on average for seventy-one litigations.[30]

2.3.2.7 Pac-Man Defence

Pac-Man defence is a corporate strategy designed to repel an unfriendly takeover, named after the eponymous video game Pac-Man. The term "Pac-Man Defence" has been accredited to Bruce Wasserstein, Chairman and CEO of Lazard. In the game Pac-Man is able to turn around and eat the ghosts chasing after him in the maze, as soon as he got a power pellet. Analogue to the game, the defence strategy implies that the subject of the bid, the target company, "turns around" and tries to take over the original predator.[31]

2.3.2.8 Suicide Pill

The suicide pill is an extreme version of the poison pill, also known as Jonestown defence. It refers to the 1987 Jonestown mass suicide in Guyana, where Jim Jones led the members of the Peoples Temple (a religious cult) to kill themselves. In the economic sense, Jonestown defence refers to any anti-takeover technique implemented by the target in which protection can result in self-destruction. In order to thwart the acquirer's bid the company engages in tactics (e.g. destruction of all valuable assets, etc.) that might threaten its existence. In extreme cases the scorched earth policy, originally a military strategy, which involves the destruction of anything useful to the enemy, may develop into a suicide pill as well.[32]

---

[30] See Jarrell, G. A. (1985)
[31] http://www.investopedia.com/terms/p/pac-man-defense.asp (enquiry: 16.03.2009)
[32] http://www.investopedia.com/terms/s/suicidepill.asp (enquiry: 16.03.2009)

Summary overview of common post-bid defence strategies

Defence Strategy	Description	Impact
Greenmail	Targeted repurchase of shares held by the potential acquirer at a substantial premium.	Elimination of a potential bidder.
Standstill agreement	Limitation of the potential bidder's holding in the target for a specified period of time.	Elimination of a potential bidder. Extended time frame for implementation of other defence measures.
Asset restructuring	Modifications of the target's asset structure, such as: a) Divestiture of assets the bidder would like to exploit (e.g. disposal of key assets, also known as "crown jewel defence") b) Purchase of assets the bidder does not want c) Buying of assets that are likely to trigger regulatory problems	Makes the target less attractive. Reduction of the target company's value.
Liability restructuring	Involves measures such as: a) Issuance of shares to a friendly third party or increase of shareholders b) Repurchase of shares at a premium from existing shareholders c) Leveraged recapitalization	Makes it more difficult for a hostile bidder to obtain the number of shares required to gain control over the target Makes the target less attractive.
White Knight	The target prefers to be acquired by a friendly third party.	Elimination of a potential bidder.
Litigation	Lawsuits filed against the bidder for various reasons (e.g. violation of anti-trust or security laws).	Delays the bidder. Encourages other bidders to launch competing offers.
Pac-Man Defence	The target company turns around and launches a takeover offer for its original bidder.	Elimination of a potential bidder.
Suicide pill	Extreme version of the poison pill, in which the target's anti-takeover measure results in self-destruction.	Elimination of a potential bidder, in the worst-case scenario the target is destroyed itself.

Table 4: Summary of post-bid defence strategies
Source: Adapted from Ruback, R. S. (1988), p. 62

2.4 Latest Development and Outlook

Over the past three years dealmakers have enjoyed an unprecedented deal boom. However, in 2007 warning signs became increasingly apparent as losses began to mount on sub prime loans and the one-booming housing market began to weaken. Already in July 2007 the Investment bank Bear Sterns had announced the virtual collapse of two hedge funds with losses of approximately USD 1.5 billion after because of failed transactions relating to sub prime mortgage securities and other credit instruments. Amid fears about their own balance sheets banks started to hoard cash and as a consequence the once-abundant flows of cheap credit started to dry up. Widely the announcement by the French banking giant BNP Paribas on August 9, 2007 is cited as the starting point of the global credit crunch. "The complete evaporation of liquidity in certain market segments of the U.S. securitization market has made it impossible to value certain assets fairly regardless of their quality or credit rating," the bank said in a statement.[33] At the same time central banks stepped in and pumped billions of dollars into the financial system in order to boost liquidity, the first of many such operations to come.

In March 2007 the FED, the U.S. Treasury and J.P. Morgan Chase had engineered the dramatic bailout of Bear Stearns. J.P. Morgan bought it's rival for just USD 2 per share and the FED provided up to USD 30 billion in financing for Bear Stearn's less-liquid assets. Concerns over the health of major financial institutions continually mounted, accompanied by the deterioration of credit market conditions. Further on, the U.S. government rescued the mortgage giants Fannie Mae and Freddie Mac with combined losses of USD 14 billion by pledging to invest approximately USD 100 billion in each to keep them solvent. On September 15, 2008 Lehman Brothers, one of the most prestigious investment banks, ranking among the top 5 institutions, filed for chapter 11 bankruptcy protection. At the same time Merrill Lynch agreed to be taken over by Bank of America in a USD 50 billion all-stock deal, as it feared a collapse.[34] The transformation of Goldman Sachs and Morgan Stanley, the last big independent investment banks on Wall Street, to bank holding companies marked the end of an era of high finance that had defined the modern gilded age.[35] In an effort to quell the global financial turmoil, the FED, the ECB, the Bank of England as well as other central banks from Canada, Switzerland and

---

[33] http://news.bbc.co.uk/2/hi/business/6938425.stm (enquiry: 17.03.2009)
[34] See Watts, W. L. (2009)
[35] See Sorkin, A. R., Bajaj, V. (2008)

Sweden simultaneously announced a coordinated plan to cut key interest rates. Equities, however, continued to plunge and central banks kept responding with interest rate cuts. At the end of 2008 U.S. interest rates were cut from an already 50-year low of 1 percent to between zero and 0.25 percent. This aggressive measure was taken in order to stave off a recession and deflation. For the same reason the Bank of England had slashed the UK base rate to 0.5 percent in March 2009. Also the European Central Bank followed by cutting its benchmark level to a record low of 1.50 percent. As Iceland's largest banks were unable to obtain short-term funding, the government took control of the institutions, resulting in a currency collapse. The nation received a USD 2 billion standby loan from the IMF. Iceland's economy however is forecasted to suffer a severe contraction. Furthermore also Hungary, Latvia, Ukraine, Belarus and Serbia received multilateral aid. In order to prevent a massive slowdown of its rapidly growing export-focused economy China unveiled a USD 586 billion stimulus package to be spent over the next two years. But not only the previously mentioned countries are facing a severe economic slowdown. The burst of the U.S. housing bubble together with the credit crunch had triggered a global economic slowdown. Despite wide-ranging policy actions, such as government stimulus packages, the financial strains remain acute and are pulling down the real economy. According to the IMF's World Economic Outlook Update global growth (measured in purchasing-power parity) is projected to fall by 3 percent in 2009. Furthermore global GDP growth in 2009 is expected to fall to 0.5 percent, its lowest rate since World War II. The global economy is said to enter a recession for the first time since 1982. A sustained economic recovery is not rendered possible until the financial sector's functionality is rebuilt and credit markets are restored.[36]

Confidence in the M&A market had been seriously dented following the Lehman collapse and the widening market turmoil. Worldwide companies started to put many deals on ice, as the share price volatility made it harder to execute deals.[37]

---

[36]   See IMF (Ed.) (2009)
[37]   See Saigol, L., Arnold, M. (2008)

Source: Yahoo Finance, The Washington Post (2008)

Deal figures for the first half of 2008 illustrate how badly the market for mergers and acquisitions as well as for initial public offerings (IPOs) had been affected by the global credit crunch. According to Dealogic, the total deal volume in the first half of 2008 was USD 1.87 billion, representing a 30 percent decrease in contrast to the equal period in 2007. This was the slowest start to a year since 2005. This slump largely is the result of a declining activity in the private equity sector, as private equity houses are facing severe problems in obtaining leveraged funding. Private equity buyouts were worst affected by the global financial crisis, as their share in total M&A volume melted down from 20 percent in 2007 to only 7 percent in 2008. With a decrease in deal activity of 60 percent in the first half, compared to a global fall of 35 percent, UK's M&A market had been worst affected.[38] Also the global IPO market has suffered a severe decline due to the financial crisis. According to Thomson Reuters 96 companies worldwide had cancelled their IPO, compared to 41 IPO-cancellations in the same period in 2007. In the first half of 2008 the number of IPOs plunged from 729 in the first six months in 2007 to only 285, representing a decrease of approximately 60 percent.[39]

Analysts from BernsteinResearch predict the M&A volume to fall 25 percent in 2009 and decrease another 15 percent in 2010. "This means that we expect a peak-to-trough decline in announced M&A volumes [over

---

[38] See Seib, C. (2008)
[39] See Neue Züricher Zeitung (Ed.) (2008)

28

2007 to 2010] of 45%, driven by a 53% decline in financial sponsor volumes and a 40% decline in strategic volumes. As a comparison, we saw volumes decline about 70% peak-to-trough over 2000-03," Brad Hintz from BernsteinResearch reports[40].

The economic outlook for 2009 is one of the most challenging for many years, but can also provide significant opportunities for investors. The law firm DibbsBarker sees investment and acquisition occasions especially for small and medium enterprises (SME) and mid market private equity. Whilst larger deals (with except scrip offers) and top-end private equity will not be able to generally attract leveraged funding at acceptable rates of return for investors, SMEs mostly rely on less debt and more cash. In the short-term distressed asset funds, mid market private equity as well as cash rich corporates are perceived to be best placed for M&A activity in 2009 and 2010.[41]

---

[40] See The Wall Street Journal (Ed.) (2008)
[41] See Schmidt-Uili, P., Cairns, G., McFarlane, A. (2009)

3 Empirical Research

3.1 Research Approach

The purpose of the study conducted within the frame of this thesis is to analyze a sample of 335 hostile takeover bids, sourced from the deal intelligence provider mergermarket, in order to determine the defence strategies applied in a first step. Further on the statistical findings will serve as a basis for evaluating the effectiveness of the utilized measures and understanding possible patterns of behaviour.

In order to preserve a structured approach and at the best possible rate achieve the goals set in this paper the following two research questions have been developed to serve as guidance when collecting, processing and analyzing the data:

1. **Which defence tactics have been most frequently applied by target companies and why?**
2. **What effect did the chosen anti-takeover defences have on the hostile takeover bid?**

For an effective and focused analytic procedure the underlying sample for this study is defined in terms of three dimensions:

- **Area coverage:** The geographic focus of this study is unlimited, or in other words, this study aims at providing a global perspective on hostile takeover defence, without regional restrictions. The global approach was chosen in order to provide an overall perspective on anti-takeover measures. In this context it has to be noted that specific measures are not applicable in certain countries due to a varying legal environment. However, this does not affect the purpose of this study, as anti-takeover strategies prohibited by a country's legislation will not be installed beforehand because of a lack of feasibility and therefore non-existent protection in case of emergency. This worldwide study of takeover defence in hostile situations contains valuable insights, as it pictures common practice in takeover defence on a global basis.

- **Time period:** The period under review is limited to six years, reaching from January 1, 2003 to December 31, 2008, triggered by the announcement date of the hostile takeover bid. Only transactions that have been announced within this defined period of time will be included in the study. Six years seem to be an adequate time frame allowing the observation of longer-term development and major trends in defence strategies. Furthermore this study aims at providing a more current view on takeover defence, as since the 1980s anti-takeover defence has undergone several developments and has become more sophisticated during the last decade.

- **Deal nature:** This dimension relates to the segmentation of deals applied within the database mergermarket. As this study solely focuses on hostile takeover bids only transactions classified as "contested, hostile", "contested, white knight" and "unsolicited, hostile" are considered within the analysis. These classifications represent the total spectrum of available data on hostile takeovers within mergermarket. A deal is described as "contested, hostile" when there is more than one bidder and the proposal is hostile, whereas the classification "unsolicited, hostile" applies to deals not recommended by the target's management within two weeks after announcement. When a company that is subject to a contested hostile bid seeks a friendly merger with a third party to fend off the hostile bidder the deal is categorized as "contested, white knight".[42]

The geographic definition, time restriction and deal nature selection are the only limitations to the sample used for the empirical study. All transactions meeting the above defined restriction criteria are subject of the empirical study, irrespective of the deal status, transaction volume or other criteria. There are no other conditions upon which a hostile takeover bid had been included or excluded from the sample.

3.2 Sample

As previously mentioned, the study examines hostile takeover bids for target companies worldwide listed on global exchanges that were announced in the time period from 1998 to 2008. The data sample was drawn from mergermarket, an independent M&A intelligence service, monitoring public as well as private M&A deals worldwide. The database covers European deals greater than EUR 5 million since 1998, all American deals greater than USD 5 million since 2001 and all Asia-Pacific deals greater than USD 5 million since 2003.[43] A detailed list of the sample deals is available upon request.

---

[42] http://www.mergermarket.com/home/glossary.asp (enquiry: 16.03.2009)
[43] http://www.mergermarket.com/ (enquiry: 16.03.2009)

The sample underlying the empirical study is determined by the following query, defined according to the scope of the analysis:

- Target/seller details and bidder details: all industry sectors and all geographic regions have been selected

- Data range: from "01/01/2003" to "31/12/2008"

- Nature of deal: "contested, hostile", "contested, white knight" and "unsolicited, hostile" have been selected

Even though the existence of alternative deal intelligence providers apart from mergermarket (e.g. Bloomberg, Reuters, Thomson Financial, etc.), the use of different data sources for the compilation of this study has been purposely avoided because of variances in definitions and calculation bases. For preventing contradictions and misleading conclusions the information used in the empirical part is restricted to deal intelligence derived from mergermarket. The database is used as source for financial information, deal structure, terms, conditions etc. It is important to note that the study fully relies on the correctness and accuracy of the data quality provided by mergermarket, no verification or cross-checking has been performed. Deal intelligence derived from the database has been used as a primary source of information. As a second source annual reports as well as other company specific information (e.g. company websites, newsletters, etc.) have been considered to obtain information not available in the database in order to ensure completeness. Whenever data was available from both sources (mergermarket and annual reports) the information is generally taken from mergermarket to provide a more consistent data definition and interpretation across different transactions and companies. Nevertheless, in the case of obviously contradicting data between the two sources, annual reports are preferred because they are considered to be more reliable and more accurate.

3.3 Definitions and Terminology

This section shortly outlines the general terminology and definitions used in alphabetical order and shall furthermore serve as an overview of the industry codes applied within the scope of the study. Additional definitions beyond the ones listed below that apply to annual reports or other specific terminology of the respective company will be highlighted in their context.

- **Announcement Date:** The date at which the hostile takeover bid was publicly announced. It is used as a point of reference to differentiate between the pre-bid announcement and the post-bid announcement period. This distinction is vital to allocate the applied defence strategies in a next step.

- **Country:** Description of the country where the respective company is incorporated by law. For a more top-level perspective countries are grouped to regions (can be either Europe, North America, South America, Asia, Africa or Australia).

- **Deal status:** Description of the current transaction status, which can be either "pending", "completed" or "terminated"

- **Hostile:** Description of the nature of the bid (can be either "contested, hostile", "contested, white knight" or "unsolicited, hostile"), whereby a hostile transaction is generally defined as one in which the first received offer is opposed by the target's management and board of directors.

- **Raider:** Name of the legal entity, which is initiated the hostile takeover bid, i.e. e. which acts as bidder or potential acquirer

- **Target:** Name of the legal entity, which is the addressee or recipient of the hostile takeover bid, i.e. which shall be acquired

Industry Sector	Description
Automotive & Assembly	Companies engaged in manufacture or distribution of automotive components (parts, accessories, including tires and rubber) as well as vehicle manufacturers (passenger vehicles, light and heavy duty trucks, motorcycles, scooters and other three wheelers and earthmoving construction vehicles);
Consumer & Retail	Manufacturers, suppliers and retailers with a focus on consumer goods and services;
Financial Services	Companies involved in banking, fund management, brokerage, principal finance, rental and leasing, securities and commodity brokerage, including venture capital firms, private equity houses and REITs;
Media & Telecommunications	Media comprises media houses providing multimedia activities as well as companies engaged in advertising, publishing, TV and radio broadcast;
	Telecommunications relates to carriers of cable telecom, fixed line telecom and mobile/satellite telecom services and also includes manufacturers of telecom equipment (e.g. voice and data communication equipment, etc.);
Leisure	Category summarizing owners and operators of hotels, guesthouses, motels as well as restaurants, pubs and other entertainment (e.g. cinemas, casinos, theme parks, etc.);
High Tech	Manufacturers and distributors of computer soft- and hardware as well as companies providing semiconductors and other electronic components; Internet and E-commerce;
Travel, Infrastructure & Logistics	Companies operating in the field of transportation (airlines, airports, freight and other transportation services, railways, mail and package shipment, etc.), infrastructure and travel (tour operators, travel agencies);
Utilities	Operators of coal-fired power stations, companies engaged in oil and gas exploration and production, businesses active in electrical power generation/transmission, energy conservation as well as companies involved in diversified activities in the electricity, water and gas sub industries;
Services	Providers of business support services, consulting and engineering services;
Industrial	Category summarizing aluminium and raw material production, industrial equipment, electronics and machinery, iron and steel production, pollution and recycling related services, manufacturers and suppliers of pumps, compressors, rail stock, refrigeration equipment, etc.
Pharma & Healthcare	Health institutions, medical service providers, manufacturers of medical equipment, handicap aids and basic healthcare supplies; Companies engaged in researching, developing, manufacturing and supplying drugs;
Materials & Mining	Companies mining for metal ore and non-metallic minerals; businesses active in construction as well as manufacturers of construction materials and chemicals;

Table 5: Industry Description
Source: Compiled by the author

4   Empirical Results

4.1 Statistical Findings

4.1.1 Development Over Time

The following graph relates to the development of hostile activity during the sixth merger wave. It illustrates the breakdown of the underlying sample by years in terms of number of bids as well as in terms of deal volume during the period under review.

Exhibit 7: Development over time

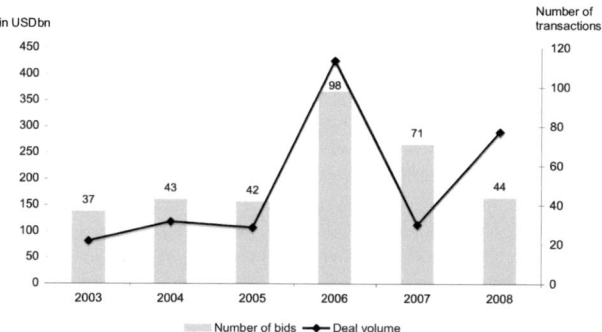

Source: Complied by the author

At the beginning of the sixth merger wave, hostile activity remained at quite the same level in terms of announced bids. In 2004 the number of announced bids had risen by six from 37 to 43, accounting for a 16 percent increase. Deal volume in the same time frame however, had experienced a steeper development. It had soared from USD 82 billion to USD 118 billion. The raise in transaction volume of 44.5 percent from 2003 to 2004 had been followed by a 9.3 percent reduction in 2005, when the number of hostile takeover offers had decreased only by one. In the period between 2005 and 2006 the number of unfriendly takeover attempts had dramatically surged from 42 to a peak of 98 offers. This 133 percent raise in hostile bids had boosted transaction volume from 107 to a high of USD 415 billion, accounting for a 287 percent year on year increase. Consequently, hostile activity during the sixth merger wave had experienced its peak in 2006, in terms of volume as well as in terms of launched bids. The subsequent years had been characterized by a downward trend as the number of takeover attempts first plunged to 71 in 2007 and then decreased again by 38 percent to 44 bids in 2008, almost on a level with 2004. Transaction volume dipped at USD 113 billion in 2007. Nevertheless the development picked up speed again in 2008 and increased by 155 percent to USD 289 billion, reaching the second highest amount.

4.1.2 Geographic Distribution

4.1.2.1 Breakdown by Regions

For reasons of simplification countries (by incorporation of targets) have been grouped to six regions, North America, South America, Africa, Europe, Asia and Australia & Oceania. Each market's corporate financial system has its own particular characteristics due to cultural, political, legal and regulatory differences. Much of them stem from distinctions in the nature of legal obligations that managers have to the financiers as well as from differences in how courts interpret and enforce these obligations.

Exhibit 8: Breakdown by regions

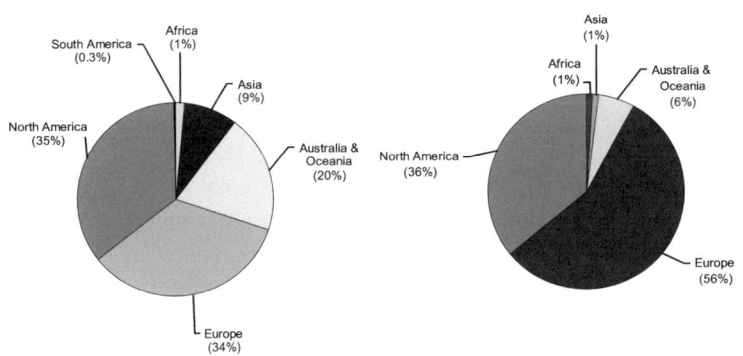

Source: Compiled by the author

In terms of announced bids, most hostile takeovers take place in North America and Europe, both together comprising approximately two thirds of the activity. The countries that experienced the most cases of hostile takeover bids are the U.S. (69), Australia (59), Canada (45) and Great Britain (34). It is commonly known that Anglo-Saxon countries are perceived to have more developed financial markets with in turn has a positive influence on the shareholder value approach. Due to the opinion of many practitioners the absence of the market of corporate control in most European countries is attributable to the structure of financial markets, with small numbers of quoted companies and ownership being concentrated in the hands of handpicked investors. Australia and Oceania ranks second with 20 percent, followed by Asia with 9 percent of the total unfriendly takeover attempts. Here Japan ranks first with 12 cases of hostile bids, accounting for a share of 40 percent of Asia's hostile bids. The remaining percentage of launched bids is distributed between Africa and South America.

By deal volume the dominance of North America and Europe becomes even more obviously. Their combined transaction volume of USD 1.03 trillion accounts for 92 percent of the total deal volume. Australia and Oceania ranks second with USD 68 billion volume, followed by Asia and Africa, both accounting for 1 percent. With USD 13.1 billion Asia's volume is slightly higher than in Africa, where the total deal value accounted for USD 8.3 billion

4.1.2.2 Cross-Border vs. Domestic Transactions

Cross-border transactions are defined as cases where the country of incorporation of the target is not identical with the bidder's country of incorporation. In contrast, domestic transactions are cases where the target and the raider have the same country of incorporation.

The ratio of cross-boarder deals to domestic deals is illustrated in exhibit 11 by two dimensions. The split by number of hostile bids launched is totally contraire to the analysis by transaction volume. In the period under review 206 domestic deals had been announced in contrast to only 129 cross-boarder transactions. As a consequence, domestic deals dominate cross-border transactions with 61 percent by the number of bids, however this dominance seems rather weak.

The analysis by deal volume in opposition shows a total controversial picture. Here cross-boarder transactions dominate domestic M&A activity with a stake of 60 percent, accounting for USD 679.3 billion. Domestic deals amount to USD 444.7 billion representing a stake of 40 percent.

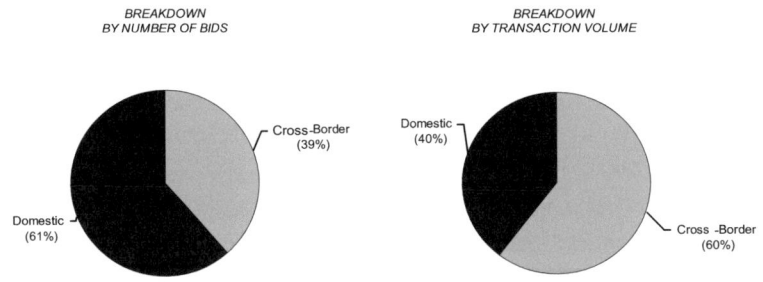

Source: Compiled by author

This outcome partly reflects the conclusion found by T. M. Zaugg (2005) in a study focusing on hostile takeover transactions in Europe in the time period from 1997 to 2001. She finds that domestic transactions dominate crossborder transactions with 66 percent in terms of number of bids and 58 percent in terms of volume.[44] The total contraire picture of the transaction breakdown by volume found by the research conducted within this thesis can be explained through its worldwide scope and the striking involvement of international private equity firms in international large-volume transactions.

4.1.3 Sector Distribution

4.1.3.1 Breakdown by Industrial Sectors

Within the scope of this thesis companies were segmented into the twelve industries Automotive & Assembly, Consumer & Retail, Financial Services, High Tech, Industrial, Leisure, Materials & Mining, Media & Telecommunication, Pharma & Healthcare, Services, Travel, Infrastructure & Logistics and Utilities (see table 5 in section 3.3.).

Exhibit 12 shows the breakdown of the sample by industrial sectors in terms of number of bids. By distinguishing between target industries and bidder industries the striking involvement of private equity firms becomes obvious. With 141 launched hostile bids the Financial Services sector

---

[44] Zaugg, M., T. (2005), p. 147

clearly ranks first, accounting for 42 percent of all bidding companies in the period under review. This finding is not surprising, as a recent study conducted by the Boston Consulting Group found that one quarter of all deals in the time period from 2003 to 2006 had been performed by the private equity sector.[45] Furthermore the conclusion above is in line with research focused on the Swedish market for corporate control performed by Johansson and Torstensson (2008). According to their analysis Private Equity (28 percent) and Financial Services (22 percent) had launched the most hostile takeover bids in the period 1997 to 2007.[46]

Most targeted industries in terms of number of bids had been Materials & Mining and Financial Services, with each 16 percent, followed by Industrial (11 percent) and Pharma & Healthcare (10 percent). The rather larger industry variances between targets and raiders indicate a light dominance of inter-sector transactions. The study by Johansson and Torstensson (2008) of the Swedish market reports similar percentages for the target segments Financials (19 percent) and Pharma & Healthcare (6 percent).[47]

Exhibit 10: Breakdown by industry

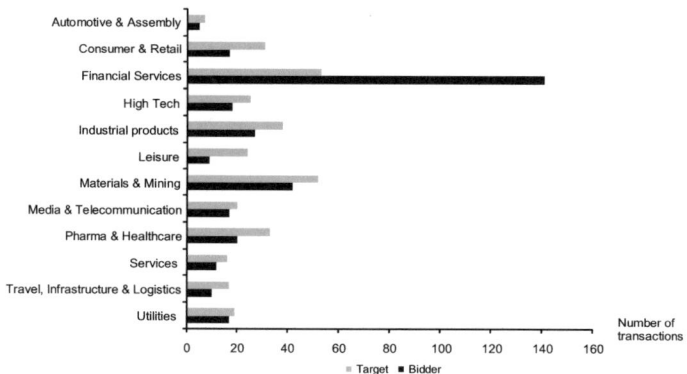

Source: Compilation by the author

In terms of volume the industrial sector Materials & Mining leads the table with USD 330.8 billion, followed by Utilities (USD 181.8 billion), Pharma & Healthcare (USD 107.4 billion) and Industrial (USD 101.7 billion). The Fi-

---

[45] See Cools, K., Gll, J., Kengelbach, J., Roos, a. (2007), p. 9
[46] See Johansson, M., Torstensson, M. (2008), p. 22
[47] See Johansson, M., Torstensson, M. (2008), p. 24

nancial Services industry, dominating in terms of launched hostile bids only ranks seventh with a volume of USD 87.2 billion, representing a stake of 8 percent. The three leading industries Materials & Mining (29 percent), Utilities (16 percent) and Pharma & Healthcare (10 percent) combined represent more than 50 percent of the total transaction volume in the period under review.

Without going into details by analyzing P/E ratios and other trading multiples of specific transactions, the ranking difference in terms of announced bids and deal volume indicates the existence of large variances in valuation approaches across industries. For instance, Financial Services ranked first in terms of launched bids, but was rather on the low end in terms of transaction volume. In contrast the Utilities sector had only seen 19 bids, however it is one of the largest by volume. Materials and Mining is ranked ex aequo with the Financial Services industry but accounts for approximately the fourfold volume.

A possible driver for the high activity in the sectors Materials & Mining and Utilities is industry consolidation, dominating the entire sixth merger wave. Furthermore certain industries are facing a more liberal regulatory environment. The boost in hostile activity in the utility sector stems from the U.S. government's decision to repeal the Public Utility Holding Company Act 1995, resulting in greater financial freedom and opportunities to pursue cross-regional deals.

Exhibit 11: Industrial sectors by volume

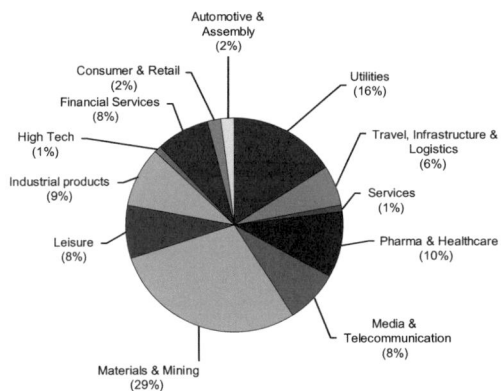

Source: Compiled by the author

4.1.3.2 Inter-Sector vs. Intra-Sector Transactions

Cases where the industrial sector of the target company is not the same as the industrial sector of the potential acquirer are defined as inter-sectoral transactions. In contrast deals where the corporate raider and the target company are both active in the same industry are classified as intra-sectoral.

As visualized in exhibit 12 intra-sector transactions dominate inter-sector transactions, whereby the dominance is quite pronounced both in terms of number of bids (57 percent) as well as in terms of volume (74 percent).

A more detailed evaluation of intra-sector transactions reveals that a majority of 64.3 percent involve a financial investor as raider targeting a non-financial company. However, considering the total deal sample these cases only represent a 27.5 stake. Consequently, it can be stated that industrial raiders clearly outweigh the cases of financial predators by a ratio of 3:1. This finding implies that industrial competitors might be in a better situation to evaluate their peers and perform a suitable valuation of the potential target.

According to Zaugg (2005) the European market in the time period from 1997 to 2001 depicts an even stronger dominance of intra-sectoral transactions, in terms of launched hostile bids (73 percent) as well as by volume (99 percent).

Exhibit 12: Inter-sector vs. intra-sector transactions

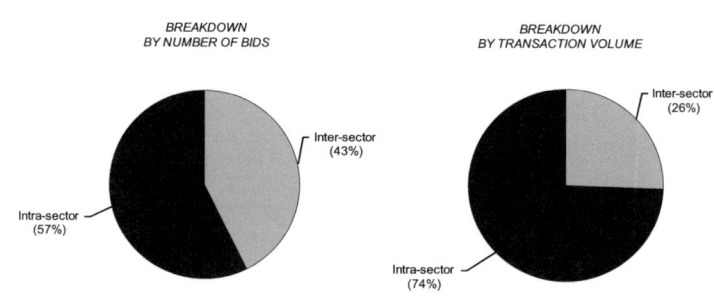

Source: Complied by the author

4.1.4 Transaction Volume

As outlined in section 3.1. the underlying sample comprises a total of 335 hostile takeover bids launched in the time period from 2003 to 2008. The total transaction value of these 335 hostile takeovers accounts for USD 1.12 billion, whereby no volume data has been available for 85 cases. The table below lists the largest hostile takeover attempts by volume launched during the sixth merger wave.

Deal volume (in USDbn)	Target	Bidder	Year	Deal status
190.34	Rio Tinto plc	BHP Billiton Ltd	2008	Terminated
73.04	Endesa SA	E.ON AG	2006	Terminated
66.00	The Walt Disney Company	Comcast Corporation	2004	Terminated
58.92	Anheuser-Busch Companies Inc	InBev SA	2008	Completed
52.29	Endesa SA	Gas Natural SDG SA	2005	Terminated
37.87	Arcelor SA	Mittal Steel N.V.	2006	Completed

Table 6: Largest deals of the sixth merger wave
Source: Mergermarket

As shown in table 6 the targeted corporations are all among the well-established top-players in their industry and home market. This fact indicates that company size is no protection against hostile takeover approaches. However, only two of the five largest attempts during the sixth merger wave have been completed.

The breakdown of hostile takeover bids by transaction size in terms of number of bids indicates that most announced offers (29.6 percent) were in the range of USD 100 million to USD 499 million, adding up to a total volume of USD 215.15 billion. Furthermore 23.6 percent of the launched bids had a transaction value of above USD 1 billion. Hostile takeover offers with a value of below USD 100 million made up one fourth of the total sample bids, representing only 0.3 percent of the total transaction value. In 21 cases offers above USD 10 billion had been made. These 19 potential deals with an announced value of above USD 10 billion made up 53.9 percent (USD 606.1 billion) of the total sample volume.

Comparing the outcome of this thesis' research with results found by Zaugg (2005) it can be stated that the breakdown by transaction size for the European market does not differ from the global perspective. The analysis with a focus on Europe also found the majority of transactions

(29.7 percent) to be in the range of USD 100 million to USD 499 million, reflecting the worldwide trend found in the present study.[48]

Exhibit 13: Breakdown by transaction size

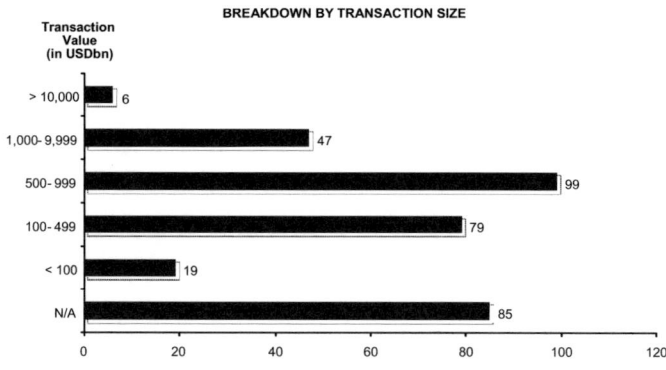

Source: Compiled by the author

4.1.5 Transaction Outcome

The aim of the analysis of transaction outcomes is to gain a view on the success rate of corporate raiders to convince the target's shareholders to sell their shares. In accordance with the database mergermarket three possible deal status classifications, have been defined:

- **Completed:** This status indicates that the particular deal is no longer subject to any approvals and has been consummated. The underlying sample contains 134 completed transactions adding up to a total deal volume of USD 326.4 billion.

- **Terminated:** This status indicates that the deal has been dissolved and will no longer continue. The derived data sample includes 183 cases with a total transaction volume of USD 794.6 billion that had been flagged with the deal status "terminated".

- **Pending:** This status describes a still active deal awaiting completion or termination. The analyzed sample comprises 18 pending hostile takeover deals accounting for a deal volume of USD 3.1 billion.

---

[48]   See Zaugg, M., T. (2005), p. 138

The following graph illustrates the breakdown of transactions by deal status along two dimensions, firstly by number of announced bids and secondly by deal volume.

Exhibit 14: Breakdown by transaction outcome

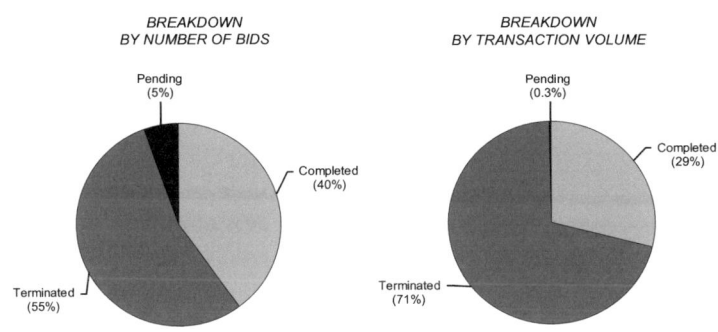

Source: Compiled by the author

In terms of announced hostile takeover offers 55 percent of all bids had been terminated, while 134 transactions accounting for 40 percent had been completed. The 18 still active transactions accounting for a five percent share are yet subject to the completion of a due diligence investigation, the availability for financing for the transaction or approval by the target company's board of directors and shareholders or regulatory authorities. As a matter of fact, businesses have been rather successful in warding off corporate raiders.

By volume more than two thirds of the unfriendly takeover proposals have been terminated. The split 71 percent of lapsed hostile takeovers versus 29 percent of completed deals reflects the fact that the failed takeovers had been rather large in size. This finding is in line with table 6 listing the largest hostiles in terms of volume, whereby four out of six takeovers had failed. This implies that target companies rather large in size had been more capable of preserving independence than smaller companies.

The study by Zaugg (2005) on the European market distinguishes between the following three possible outcomes for transactions: completed and acquired, terminated and independent and terminated and acquired. The study basically shows a similar outcome with 39 percent completed transactions and 61 percent terminated transactions in terms of launched bids. The breakdown by volume however is contraire to the global view-point found in this study. In Europe, measured by volume, 68 percent of all transactions had been completed and 32 percent had been termi-nated.[49]

4.1.6 Defence Strategy

The evaluation of the general defence strategy approach (see exhibit 17) found that out of 55 percent of the target companies (184 targets) that had installed a defence system, 15 percent had applied pre-offer anti-takeover defences, 82 percent tried to ward off the raider by post-bid de-fence and only a minority of 3 percent had pursued a combined defence strategy to preserve independence. From a top-level perspective based on the total sample of 335 transactions it can be stated that in 151 cases (45 percent) the target did not implement any defence measures; most often the board of directors only gave a recommendation to its share-holders. The majority of unfriendly approached companies accounting for 55 percent had chosen to initiate anti-takeover proceedings.

Exhibit 15: General defence approach

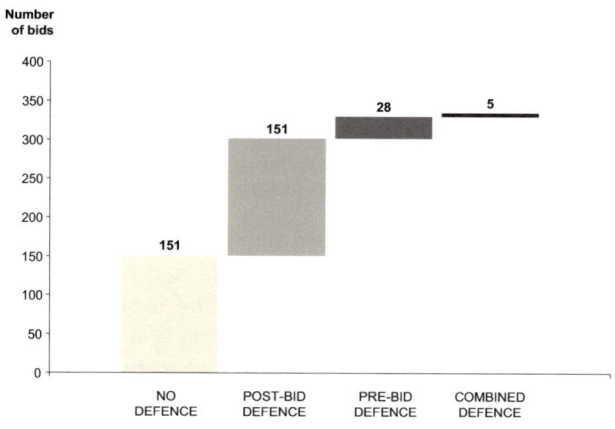

Source: Compiled by the author

---

[49]   See Zaugg, M., T. (2005), p. 142

4.1.6.1 Pre-Bid Defence

As described in chapter 2.3.1 pre-bid defences are proactive measures in-stalled prior to the receipt of a takeover offer. In the underlying sample 9.6 percent of all target companies had erected such pre-offer takeover barriers. Table 7 lists the applied anti-takeover measures and the fre-quency of their implementation. The success rate indicates which per-centage of hostile bids could be terminated depending on the specific de-fence measure. The analysis is based on the completed and terminated transactions of the sample, pending offers had not been included.

Cases	Pre-bid defence	Success rate
26	Poison pill	50%
4	Restricted voting rights	75%
1	Super-majority provision	0%
1	Golden parachute	100%
1	Dual class stock	100%
1	Staggered board	0%

Table 7: Pre-bid defence
Source: Compiled by the author

The most frequent defence had been the poison pill, applied in 26 cases with a success rate of 50 percent, i.e. 50 percent of the companies that had put this defence in place had been able to ward off the raider and stay independent. In the remaining situations the enacted poison pills had pre-served the board's bargaining power and flexibility in dealing with the hostile acquirer. They had been used as a tool to mitigate the influence of the predators, in most cases large institutions. So the targeted enter-prises had not been scooped up at a bargain price, but were able to realize more shareholder value from the acquisition. This had been rendered possible, as the raider had raised the offer price in order to persuade the board of directors to adopt the poison pill to make a transaction possible.

Four companies had amended their charters to include restricted voting rights provisions, whereby only one of these companies had been taken over. Dual class stock has been implemented in one case, with a success rate of 100 percent, as the hostile acquisition had failed. Within the sam-ple there was only found one case each for super-majority provisions, golden parachutes, dual class stock and staggered boards. It has to be pointed out that the anti-takeover defences golden parachute and super-majority provision had only been found in combination with other meas-ures (poison pills, staggered boards).

Three of the analyzed targets had installed a combination of two pre-bid measures to prevent takeovers, whereby two of these transactions have been completed.

In the case Ventana Medical Systems vs. Roche Holding the target Ventana had combined restricted voting rights with a staggered board defence. The initial unsolicited offer submitted by Roche had not been successful due to the installed pre-bid measures and effective shareholder communication. In further consequence the raider had increased the initial offer price of USD 75 per share by 19.3 percent to USD 89.5, valuing Ventana at USD 3.1 billion. Only after Roche had boosted the offer price the two companies had reached a definitive agreement. Here the prior installed anti-takeover defence had been successful, as it enabled the management board to keep control of the situation.

Wegener Corporation had installed a poison pill and in addition the company's top executives would receive a lump sum severance payment equal to 2.5 times salary plus bonuses received in the prior year in the case of a change in control of the company. Radyne Corporation had terminated its unsolicited cash offer because of the Wegener's unwillingness to redeem its poison pill and the management's refusal to rescind the golden parachutes. In this case the installed pre-bid measures had prevented a hostile acquisition and secured the target's independence.

BASF's hostile offer for Engelhard Corporation had been conditional to the inapplicability of the target's shareholder rights plan and the super-majority voting provisions. For reasons of tough market conditions and Engelhard's rather weak performance the company ultimately had no choice but to accept BASF's hostile offer.[50]

4.1.6.2 Post-Bid Defence

After receiving a hostile takeover bid companies furthermore have the possibility to defend themselves with several post-offer strategies that can be directed specifically against a particular bidder.

---

[50] www.mergermarket.com (enquiry: 13.04.2009)

Table 8 presents which defence measures had been applied in the period under review.

Cases	Post-bid defence	Success rate
57	Shareholder communication	98%
49	White knight/squire	76%
22	Litigation	77%
11	Liability restructuring	82%
5	Asset restructuring	40%
5	Dividend payment	100%
3	MBO	0%

Table 8: Post-bid defence
Source: Compiled by the author

The most frequently implemented post-bid strategies are effective shareholder communication followed by searching for a white knight and legislation, i.e. filing a lawsuit against the potential acquirer for various reasons.

The post-bid analysis has found that most companies that had been able to resist a hostile acquisition had immediately pursued effective shareholder communication. The target's management board had not just recommended shareholders not to tender their shares, but strongly attacked the logic of the potential acquirers bid. By setting the company's strong value proposition in sharp contrast to the often undervalued takeover offer shareholders had been convinced not to accept the offer. In 57 out of 58 cases of application the raider did not achieve the minimum acceptance rate and therefore the hostile bid had been terminated.

In 49 hostile situations the target companies sought a white knight/squire, i.e. 26.6 percent of all companies that had implemented anti-takeover defence at all had tried to avoid a hostile acquisition by entering an agreement with a friendly third party. In fact, 37 target companies managed to avoid an unfriendly acquisition, resulting in a success rate of 75 percent.

Furthermore, litigation ranks among the top three strategies with a high success rate of 77 percent. Out of 22 cases where target companies filed lawsuits against their raiders for reasons like violation of anti-trust or securities regulations only 5 had been completed. By looking at the completed transactions however, the tenderers had raised their offers for reasons of avoiding further legal expenses and inducing the target to drop the suit.

The category liability restructuring relates to all measures having an impact on the target's capital structure, such as share buy-backs or the issuance of new shares. In 11 hostile situations the target companies had undergone liability restructuring for defending themselves against the predator. Only one enterprise that had chosen such measures as a post-offer defence strategy had been acquired. Therefore the success of measures regarding the enterprise's capital structure is relatively high and accounts for 82 percent.

In order to remain independent 5 companies had chosen to sell their crown jewels and other valuable assets that might have been of interest to the bidder. In spite of undergoing a major asset restructuring 60 percent of the targets that had implemented this measure had been acquired. This finding is rather surprising, as in general it is assumed that the spin off of valuable resources the predator wishes to exploit drastically reduces the target's attractiveness. In spite of the previous mentioned however, the majority of hostile approaches had been completed.

The analysis found that extraordinary high dividend payment to shareholders is a very effective strategy to ward off corporate raiders, as all five targets succeeded in their defence. This is firstly due to the fact that an increased dividend payment discourages shareholders from selling their stake in the target company and makes it more difficult for the raider to gain a controlling interest. Moreover huge dividend payments drain all the cash on hand and therefore reduce the target's attractiveness.

In the period under review three companies tried to resolve their hostile takeover situation by a Management Buy Out (MBO). However, not one single MBO succeeded, therefore resulting in a success rate of zero percent. In all cases shareholders had tendered their shares to the corporate raiders.

In general the findings of this thesis are supported by Johansson and Torstensson, who have found "Attack the logic of the bid" (56.3 percent) and "Positive Publics Info" (28.1 percent) to be the most frequently applied defence measures in the Swedish market. Basically these two categories established by Johansson Torstensson can be considered as the post-bid measure "Shareholder communication" used within the frame of this thesis. The fact that the white knight defence and litigation rank among the widely used strategies is not surprising, as they are characterized by great effectiveness and efficiency. Also Johansson and Torstensson find the

previously mentioned defence approaches to be among the most frequent in Sweden.[51]

4.1.6.3 Combined Strategy

In this section the combined defence approach has been evaluated, i.e.
the cases in which targeted companies had already installed pre-bid
measures and in addition proactively defended themselves against the
predator. In the underlying sample five companies had implemented this
two-dimensional strategy. This accounts for a minority share of 2.7 percent of all companies that had implemented anti-takeover defence.
Table 9 below illustrates the combinations applied.

Cases	Pre-bid defence	Post-bid defence	Success rate
2	Poison pill	White knight	50%
1	Poison pill	Asset restructuring	100%
1	Restricted voting rights	Liability restructuring	100%
1	Restricted voting rights	Litigation	100%

Table 9: Combined defence strategy
Source: Compiled by the author

Three companies that had been approached by a hostile bidder had installed poison pills prior to the offer. In addition one target sold its crown
jewels and therefore could successfully prevent a hostile takeover. The
other two targets actively sought a white knight in order to prevent the
acquisition. One company had adopted its shareholder rights plan to en-
able a friendly merger with the white knight and therefore successfully
warded off the predator. In the other case the hostile transaction had
been completed, as the offer had been steadily raised until the target's
board had approved the transaction. Similar to the completed transactions in section 4.2.6.1. the unfriendly approached enterprise had been
able to keep control of the situation and prompted the predator to raise
its bid to an appropriate and acceptable level.

Restricted voting rights provisions had been found in combination with
liability restructuring and litigation. Both of these integrated approaches
had been successful in avoiding the hostile transaction. As each of these
measures is highly effective on a standalone basis, the success of a combined implementation is not surprising.

---

[51] See Johansson, M., Torstensson, M. (2008), p. 26

Compared to the study by Johansson and Torstensson it must be pointed out that the combined strategy approach is far more common. However within this thesis a combined approach is defined as the joint application of pre- and post-bid defence, whereas Johansson and Torstensson have a broader definition of a combined defence-strategy. Within their study also the implementation of two post-bid tactics is summarized under a combined approach, resulting in a much higher percentage for this category. They found that approximately 35 percent of all Swedish targets had applied at least two defence strategies to ward off corporate raiders. More than two thirds of the Swedish targets that had applied more than one measure had succeeded in preserving their independence.[52]

---

[52]   See Johansson, M., Torstensson, M. (2008), p. 27

5 Final Conclusion

5.1 Key Findings

The purpose of this thesis was firstly to provide an overall perspective on common practice of anti-takeover defence measures on a global basis and in sequence investigate the effectiveness of the strategies applied. This chapter summarizes the main findings of the study and provides the answers to the two research questions that had served as guidance in collecting, processing and analyzing the data.

1. Which defence tactics had been the most frequently applied by target companies and why?

Based on the frequency of implementation most companies used post-bid defence measures (45 percent). Only 8.4 percent of all analyzed target enterprises had installed anti-takeover prevention prior to receiving the hostile bid. A minority share of 1.5 percent had pursued a combination of pre- and post-bid measures to ward off corporate raiders. In the light of the low frequency of pre-bid defences found in the underlying sample the fact that this thesis only comprises companies that had faced a hostile situation must be emphasized. As a consequence it may be the case that pre-bid defence measures are the most effective and most used, due to the fact that a successful pre-bid strategy results in no hostile takeover bid at all.

The empirical study found the following defence measures had been the most applied in the period under review: shareholder communication (57 cases), white knight (49 cases), poison pill (26 cases), litigation (22 cases) and liability restructuring (11 cases).

The rationale of maintaining effective shareholder communication concludes from its simplicity and cost effectiveness in comparison to other strategies. In the situation of receiving a hostile takeover offer attacking the logic of the bid and providing positive public information can be seen as a natural and cost efficient step by the target's management board when it deciding not to approve the offer. On a long-term basis creating an equity story, public relations and building up a strong company image are measures that effectively contribute to this measure.

The main reason for searching for a white knight is the proven efficiency of this strategy and the relatively low risk of being acquired by the raider. 26.6 percent of all companies under review that had implemented anti-takeover proceedings had chosen to rather merge with a friendly third party than to be taken over by the corporate raider.

The study found that poison pills are the most frequent applied pre-bid defence. The toxic structure of most pills had been designed in the belief that they would never be triggered. Poison pills aim at prohibitively making the company's stock less attractive to potential acquirers by making the hostile takeover more difficult and expensive.

Furthermore litigation was found to be among the frequent applied defence measures. Compliance with takeover, anti-trust and other regulations is a prerequisite for successful completing transactions. Therefore target companies encourage regulatory disputes since the raider will be exposed to the following three threats: delay in completing the transaction, competing bidders and high legal expenses.

11 targets tried to defend themselves in a hostile situation by issuing voting rights or initiating a share buyback. As a matter of fact both forms of liability restructuring are designed to make the target less attractive to the unfriendly acquirer. In the first case the number of shares required to obtain control is increased, in the second case the target pursues debt issuance as method of financing.

2. What effect did the chosen anti-takeover defences have on the hostile takeover offer?

In order to determine the effect of the chosen anti-takeover defences the ability to ward off the corporate raider had been investigated. In terms of announced hostile takeover offers 55 percent of all bids had been terminated, while a total of 134 transactions accounting for 40 percent of all transactions under review had been completed. The split 71 percent of lapsed hostile takeovers versus 29 percent of completed deals by volume reflects the fact that the failed takeovers had been rather large in size.

By focusing on the most frequently applied strategies it has to be pointed out that they all have a success rate of at least 50 percent, i.e. more than 50 percent of the target companies that had chosen the particular measure had been able to resist the hostile acquisition. The study found that ranked by success rate shareholder communication is the most successful anti-takeover defence (98 percent), followed by liability restructuring (82 percent), litigation (77 percent), white knights (76 percent) and poison pills (50 percent). These defence tactics are characterized by effectiveness and solidity.

The closer examination of the completed transactions in spite of anti-takeover measures reveals that in more than 60 percent of the cases the hostile acquirer had raised the offer price in order to close the deal. As a consequence it can be stated that defence measures have a significant influence in preserving the target's bargaining power and flexibility in dealing with hostile acquirers.

5.2 Limitations and Further Research

Hostile takeovers can be viewed from a broad spectrum of dimensions. This thesis focuses on the target company's view and its defence tools to withstand unfriendly acquisitions. However, it is also of great interest to investigate hostile situations from the raider's perspective and expand on the potential acquirer's available strategies to complete hostile transactions. In this context an analysis on the buyer's actions to cope with defence measures implemented by the target could be performed. In several cases corporate raiders increased their unsolicited bids or sweetened the takeover conditions. Nevertheless the previous envisaged analysis could provide an in-depth perspective on further possible actions to boost the probability of success of the hostile transaction.

The empirical study within the frame of this thesis determines the effectiveness of anti-takeover proceedings by deal status. However, the fact that a hostile takeover had been prevented or the transaction was completed however does not give information about positive or negative influences on shareholder value. Therefore it is essential to determine the economic effects of the defence measures applied and investigate their impact on shareholder value.

A further aim of this thesis was to give the reader a top-level perspective on defence measures. As already outlined in the previous chapter each market has particular characteristics because of cultural, political, legal and regulatory differences. These factors are important determinants of an effective defence strategy and therefore represent a further area of investigation. Moreover also industry specific trends and developments have great influence on hostile takeover activity. As a case in point the US utility sector that is now facing a more liberal regulatory environment has experienced a boost in unfriendly takeover attempts. In order to gain a detailed view of industry dynamics and understand the drivers of hostile acquisitions in certain sectors further research on an industry specific basis should be conducted.

Due to the current market turmoil caused by the financial crisis attracting leveraged funding at acceptable rates of return for investors has become a severe problem. Furthermore the LBO market dried out, stock markets lost nearly half of their values and asset values have declined across most industry sectors, leaving behind attractive investment targets. Due to this fact it will be of interest to research the behaviour of distressed asset funds, mid market private equity as well as SMEs regarding hostile take-over action as these players from a short term perspective are best placed for M&A activity during the current market situation.

6 Appendix

6.1 List of Figures

6.2 List of Tables

7   References

BAINBRIDGE, S. M. (2002): Dead Hand and No Hand Pills: Precommitment Strategies in Corporate Law, University of California, Los Angeles School of Law, Law and Economics Research Paper No. 02-02, pp. 11-13

BRUNNER, R. F. (2004): Applied Mergers and Acquisitions. Wiley, 1st edition, New Jersey.

COOLS, K., GELL, J., KENGELBACH, J., ROOS, A. (2007): The Brave New World of M&A: How to Create Value from Mergers and Acquisitions. The Boston Consulting Group, July 2007, Boston.

COPELAND, T. E., WESTON, J. F., SHASTRI K. (2005): Financial Theory and Corporate Policy. Pearson/Addison-Wesley, 4th edition, international edition, Boston.

DANN, L., Y., DEANGELO, H. (1983): Standstill Agreements, Privately Negotiated Stock Repurchases, and the Market for Corporate Control. Journal of Financial Economics, Volume 11, April, pp. 275-300.

DANN, L., Y., DEANGELO, H. (1986): Corporate Financial Policy and Corporate Control: A Study of Defensive Adjustments in Assets and Ownership Structure. Working paper 86-11, Managerial Economics Research Center of the University of Rochester, August.

FRIESWICK, K. (2001): Poison Pill Popping. In: CFO Magazine, Online October Issue, Link: http://www.cfo.com/article.cfm/3001307/1/c_3046510?f=insidecfo
(enquiry: 16.03.2009)

GAUGHAN, P. A. (2002): Mergers, Acquisitions and Corporate Restructurings. Wiley, 3rd Edition, New Jersey.

http://encyclopedia.farlex.com/Pacman+defence (enquiry: 16.03.2009)

http://www.investopedia.com/terms/p/pac-man-defense.asp (enquiry: 16.03.2009)

http://www.investopedia.com/terms/s/suicidepill.asp (enquiry: 16.03.2009)

http://www.mergermarket.com/ (enquiry: 16.03.2009)

http://www.mergermarket.com/home/glossary.asp (enquiry: 16.03.2009)

IMF (ED.) (2009): World Economic Outlook Update: Global Economic Slump Challenges Policies. Released on January 28, 2009.

Link: http://www.imf.org/external/pubs/ft/weo/2009/update/01/index.htm

(enquiry: 30.03.2009)

IVKOVIC, I. (2008a): Pre-takeover Defense Strategies: Legally Available Protective Measures Against Hostile Takeovers.

Link: http://investment-banking.suite101.com/article.cfm/pretakeover_defense
_strategies (enquiry: 16.03.2009)

IVKOVIC, I. (2008b): Post-takeover Defense Strategies: In Case Pre-takeover Defense Mechanisms Fail, Not All Is Lost.

Link: http://investment.suite101.com/article.cfm/posttakeover_defense_strategies

(enquiry: 16.03.2009)

JARRELL, G. A. (1985): The Wealth Effects of Litigating by Targets: Do Interests Diverge in a Merge?. Journal of Law and Economics, Volume 28 (April), 151-77.

JARRELL, G. A., POULSEN, A. B. (1987): Shark repellents and stock prices: The Effects of Antitakeover Amendments Since 1980. Journal of Financial Economics 19, pp. 127 – 168.

JENSEN (1988): Takeovers: Their Causes and Consequences. In: Journal of Economic Perspecitves, Winter 1988, Volume 2, No. 1, pp. 21-48.

JENSEN, M., RUBACK, R. S. (1983): The market for corporate control: The scientific evidence. Journal of Financial Economics 11, 5 – 50.

JOHANSSON, M., TORSTENSSON, M. (2008): Hostile Takeovers. The Power of the Pray. Jönköping International Business School, Sweden, May 2008, p. 22, 24, 26-27.

LAMBERT, R. A., LARCKER, D. F. (1985): Golden parachutes, executive decision-making and shareholder wealth. Journal of Accounting & Economics 7, 1985, 179 – 203.

LINN, S. C., MCCONNELL, J. J. (1983): An Empirical Investigation of the Impact of Antitakeover Amendments on Common Stock Prices. Journal of Financial Economics 11, 361-99.

LIPTON, M. (2006): Merger Waves in the 19th, 20th and 21th Centuries. The Davies Lecture, Osgoode Hall Law School, York University.

LOH, C., RATHINASAMY, R. S. (1995): Insider trading and dual-class recapitalization. Journal Of Financial And Strategic Decisions, Volume 8, Number 3.

MIKKELSON, W., RUBACK, R. S. (1986): Targeted Repurchases and Common Stock Returns. Working paper no. 1707-86, Massachusetts Institute of Technology, Sloan School of Management, June.

NELSON, R. (1959): Merger Movements in American Industry: 1895-1956. Princeton University Press, Princeton, N. J.

NEUE ZÜRICHER ZEITUNG (2008): Weniger Übernahmen und Börsegänge: Die Finanzkrise sorgt für einen Einbruch im ersteh Halbjahr. Published on July 4, 2008.

RAUPACH, G. (2007): Das M&A-Geschäft. In: Investment Banking, Hockmann, H. J., Thießen, F. (Ed.), 2nd edition, Schäffer-Poeschl, Stuttgart.

RUBACK, R. S. (1988): An Overview of Takeover Defenses. In: Alan Auerbach (Editor), Mergers and Acquisitions, University of Chicago Press, Chicago.

SAIGOL, L., ARNOLD, M. (2008): Wary companies halt M&A deals. In: Financial Times, published on September 17, 2008, Online Edition: http://www.ft.com/cms/s/0/8baeca1c-84df-11dd-b148-0000779fd18c.html?nclick_check=1 (enquiry: 30.03.2009)

SCHMIDT-UILI, P., CAIRNS, G., McFARLANE, A. (2009): M&A 2009 – an opportunity for SMEs?. Link: http://au.legalbusinessonline.com/news/features/manda-2009-an-opportunity-for-smes/34119 (enquiry: 30.03.2009)

SCHWERT, G., W. (2000): Hostility in Takeovers: In the Eyes of the Beholder?. In: The Journal of Finance, Vol. LV. No. 6, 2599-2640.

SEIB, C. (2008): Credit crunch and M&A: how the deals dried up. In: Times Online, published on August 8, 2008, Online Edition:

http://business.timesonline.co.uk/tol/business/industry_sectors/banking_and_finance/article4486857.ece (enquiry: 30.03.2009)

SORKIN, A. R., BAJAJ, V. (2008): Shift for Goldman and Morgan Marks the End of an Era. In: The New York Times, published on September 21, 2008, Online Edition:

http://www.nytimes.com/2008/09/22/business/22bank.html?hp (enquiry: 30.03.2009)

Strazzer, R. (1993): Das öffentliche Übernahmeangebot im Kapitalmarktrecht der Schweiz unter besonderer Berücksichtigung des Verhältnisses zwischen Bieter und Aktionär, Zürich.

The Wall Street Journal (Ed.) (2008): Breaking News from 2010: Reaching the Bottom Plunge. Published on December 9, 2008, Online Edition: http://blogs.wsj.com/deals/2008/12/09/breaking-news-from-2010-reaching-the-bottom-of-the-ma-revenue-plunge/ (enquiry: 30.03.2009)

The Washington Post (Ed.) (2008): Dow Jones Industrials' One-Year Dive. Published on October 8, 2008, Online Edition: http://www.washingtonpost.com/wp-dyn/content/graphic/2008/10/08/GR2008100800792.html

Watts, W. L. (2009): Milestones in the meltdown. In: MarketWatch, last updated on March 13, 2009. Link: http://www.marketwatch.com/news/story/Milestones-meltdown/story.aspx?guid={6FF3C2CA-3494-46B2-B9DA-0B121103BB14}

(enquiry: 30.03.2009)

Zaugg, M. T. (2005): The Market for Corporate Control in Europe, Impact of Hostile Take-overs on Strategic Management. Haupt Verlag, Zürich, 1. Auflage 2005, p. 138, 142, 147.